TRANSCENDING
BEYOND
YOUR
ABILITY

Ephesians 3:20

Apostle Ruth Parker

WILSON
W♔L
LEGACY
Publishers

Editors: Renee Cummings, Adrianne Wilson
Cover Design by Adrianne Wilson

TRANSCENDING BEYOND YOUR ABILITY
Copyright © 2018 by Ruth Parker
Published by Wilson Legacy Publishers
East Orange, New Jersey 07018
www.apostolicbuilders.org

ISBN-978-0-692-18811-8

Printed in the United States of America

DEDICATION

This book is dedicated to my daughter Renee J. Bradley, my son Kevin P. Parker, my sister Elder Octavia Bradberry and my brother Duranto V. Cross, all who have transitioned to the other side. I will see you again!

THANKS

To my sons Eddie and Randolph Parker, my (9) grandchildren, their wives and husbands and (14) great-grandchildren; and to the entire family and friends I thank you for all your love and support throughout the years. May the love of God continue to bless each and every one of you with long life, and good health, in Jesus' name. Amen!

TABLE OF CONTENTS

FORWARD

Our God is good all the time. People of God, I am so happy for this particular book, written by the daughter of Elohim - Apostle Ruth Parker. She is a woman of prayer and the Word of God is in her. Her passion for the things of God is serious; she has raised men and women in the kingdom of God. This book talks about one of the foundations of our journey with God, which is Faith and Faith is very vital in our lives as believers. I am happy that this book is written in line with scriptures. As believers, I believe we all need this book at this time. God bless all the readers of this incredible book.

Pastor Kwame K. Kingsley
Mizpah International Ministry
Fairfield, OH

SPECIAL RECOGNITION

Spiritual Father's

To the late Apostle Earnest Leonard, who introduced me to the Apostolic teachings, which were birthed into my spiritual womb.

To Apostle Frank Dupree, who imparted insight and understanding of my purpose as a Marketplace Apostle.

To Apostle Samuel Campbell, who heard the voice of God when I shared with him what God, by His Grace placed in my spirit to become an Apostle. He saw my potential and affirmed me as an Apostle in 2010.

To Apostle Benjamin Arazu, who guided my spiritual depth in the Word of God, which brought me into my Destiny.

Thank you all for your Impartation and Activation in my life!

Bishop Donald Hilliard Jr. - Cathedral International, Perth Amboy, NJ. What an opportunity to have served as a part of your Confirmation and to be a member of CEF/CA. Such a blessing you graced me with to speak amongst anointed men and women in your leadership team and to share how God brought me from welfare to become an entrepreneur. Thank You!

Bishop Loretta Smith-Johnson - Shekinah Glory Christian Church, Newark, NJ. Thank you, woman of God, for those informative years of my life serving as your Associate Pastor. What a great spiritual awakening. It was the beginning process of who I am today. More Grace, upon you!

The late Bishop Leroy Holmes - Resurrection Temple Church, Roselle NJ. I had the pleasure of being his Assistant Pastor for several years. He taught me about the Prison Ministry—I developed a passion for it. Years later I had the opportunity to re-open a halfway house for ex-offenders in Elizabeth, NJ. Bishop Holmes was known throughout the State of New Jersey for his dedication to prison outreach.

Pastor Jason Alvarez - Love of Jesus Family Church, Orange, N J. It was an honor to serve for seven years with you and your wife Gail at many levels from doing floors, ushering, and prayer line. Remaining faithful over those few things he will make you ruler over much. In the year of 1992 you ordained me, and I became Pastor of Jesus Cares Ministry. Thank you both, for imparting into my life.

Pastor Dorothy J. Smith - At The Cross Roads of Life Ministry, Union, NJ. You are my dear friend and sister in the Lord. I cannot thank you enough for the years you labored with me in the Gospel; from the birthing of Jesus Cares Ministry in 1992, until this present day. We have weathered many storms through the grace of God. I thank God for your prayer life that was so ever before me. Continue to stay strong in the Lord and in the Power of His might.

Pastor Renee' V. Cummings - Have God-Will Travel Ministries, Linden, NJ. Where do I start? Commitment, obedience, accountability, integrity, a humble servant, a prayer warrior who goes into battle on my behalf, a team player, a friend that I can confide in, who understands the vision God gave to me to carry out and walks with me in total agreement—all the characteristics of a Godly woman! Through the blessed times and the hard times, you have been right by my side, uplifting my arms. More Grace on your Life!

INTRODUCTION

I pray that you are richly blessed as you read this book and I thank God for His anointing, so the readers will feel His presence. I love the Word of God and the new things He is doing in my life at my age. Hearing from God is the most important part of my life. At first, I don't always understand what He is asking of me, but I've learned to be still and know that He is God. The footsteps of a righteous man are ordered by the Lord. This book is based on scripture, so you can see for yourself how I use the Word of God; may His Grace be released upon the reader.

There are no limits on what and where God can take you, so take the limits off of God. You can do all things through Christ, who gives you strength. May you be encouraged, exalted, and comforted through some of the things I have experienced.

EAGLES

The eagle is a bird of high honor in the Bible and often seen as a prophetic symbol; it displays a great freedom toward its young but can be destructive. It is noted for its ability to fly quickly to a higher altitude, (it transcends). The eagle builds his nest on a cliff or higher altitude (rocks) away from danger.

Eagles convey power and messages of the Spirit, it is man's connection to the Divine, and it flies high like no ordinary bird. When crows try to interfere with the eagles, they are unable to make a quick turn because their wings extend eight feet; therefore, they fly above to conserve energy. They learn early to soar without flapping their wings and wait for what is called a wind thermal to come upon them. A wind thermal is a big gust of wind that they can launch onto; they combine a mixture of flying and soaring on that strong wind thermal to get to where they want to go. Just as eagles learn to fly on the wind thermal, we as Born Again Spiritual Christians must learn how to fly on the power of the Holy Spirit for our lives.

From time to time eagles go through a process called molting. In this process, they lose their feathers, so that new ones can grow. This is a time of weakness and vulnerability for an eagle, and they are unable to hunt for food. But when they come through the process, they are renewed like a young bird again; but having the age and experience, they are better after going through the renewal molting process.

Isaiah 40:29-31 gives us a metaphor of an eagle's wind beneath his wings. Note: Wind and spirit comes from the same Greek word Pnuema (the soul or vital spirit). The Spirit of God lifts us up and His energy and strength sustains us as we abide in Him when we are facing difficulties. The key is learning to wait; there's no scripture that tells us to take control or fight our own battle. He gives power to the weak, and to those who have no might, He increases their strength.

Scriptures relating to eagles and their strength are: Deu. 28:49; 1 Kgs. 8:7; Psa.17, 36:7, 63:7, 91:1-4, 103; Pro. 15-16; Isa. 40:31; Lam. 4:19; Jer. 4:13, 49:22; Dan. 2:20-21; 5:18-21; Rom. 13:1-2.

Research by: Rev. Dorothy Smith

12 PRINCIPALS OF FAITH

Listed below are Twelve Principals of Faith you will see used throughout this book:

1. Obedience to Faith.
2. Faith works in your heart.
3. Faith is an action+-n that brings results.
4. If faith is not active and alive, it's not faith.
5. Faith is a spiritual force.
6. Faith is acting upon your belief in God.
7. Faith always has a destination.
8. You must release faith daily.
9. Faith brings victory.
10. Faith is what you know.
11. Faith is being committed to what God has called you to do.
12. We need to be faithful to all we have in Christ Jesus.

CHAPTER 1
MANIFESTATION OF YOUR FAITH

"Now the Lord had said unto Abram, get thee out of thy country, and from thy father's house, unto a land that I will show thee: And I will make of you a great nation, and I will bless thee and make your name great; and thou shall be a blessing." (Gen.12:1-2)

We have entered a season when God is saying "I want to do a **new thing** in you, the former things have passed, and new things do I declare; before they spring forth I tell you of them." (Isa. 42:9)

This is what God did with Abram; He said leave the land and I will shew you the new thing. It was a step of faith for Abram, just like it will be for you. But in this season, God is saying leave your father's house. This can be anything or place where you feel guarded, confined, hurt, abused—any unhealthy situation(s). If you never leave, you will never receive the promises of God. I decree and declare the New Thing upon you; God, will tell you, direct you, and provide for you. But it's all by faith!

The promises were made to Abram and his seed. The promises of faith that we have received are by the Spirit. "If you have faith as a grain of a mustard seed, you can say unto the mountain, remove hence to yonder place and it shall remove; and nothing shall be impossible unto you." (Mat. 17:20) Trusting in Jesus does not require a lot of faith.

So, what is your mountain? You must speak to the situation(s); whether it's finances, sickness, or pain, you tell the pain in your body to leave in the name of Jesus. You boldly confess that Jesus went around healing all manner of sickness and disease. "And He was wounded for your transgressions; He was bruised for your iniquities; the chastisement of your peace was upon Him; and with his stripes you are healed." (Isa. 53:5)

CONFESSIONS

Healing belongs to me just as much as salvation does; Jesus' body was broken for my physical health just as sure as His blood was shed for my sins. Therefore, I believe and boldly decree and declare that I am healed.

God your Word shall not return unto you void, but it shall accomplish that which you please and shall prosper in the things whereto you have sent it. Because you sent your Word to heal me, I return your Word to you. (Isa. 55:11)

My son attend to my Words; incline thine ear unto my sayings. Let them not depart from thine eyes; keep them in the midst of thine heart; for they are life unto those that find them, and health to all their flesh. (Pro. 4:20-22)

God, I keep your Word before me, and I meditate on your Word night and day. You said your Word is life and health to my flesh, so by faith, I declare I am healed; For I walk by faith and not by sight.

God, I am not moved by what I see, hear or feel. I am moved only by what your Word says about me. Your Word says, "by His strips I am healed." You are the Lord God that healeth thee. God, what it is, does not change who you are. I fear not, and I stagger not at your promises. No matter what the diagnosis or the symptoms, you are still the God that heals.

Now faith is confidence in what is hoped for, and assurance about what we do not see. The devil wants to keep telling you that you are still sick, there's no change in your condition. But by faith, you must believe that every sickness and disease is gone.

When Jesus went about healing with his core team Peter, James, and John, they came to a house of the ruler of the synagogue and saw the tumult (disorder) in them that wept and wailed greatly. Jesus asked them "why make ye this ado, and weep? The damsel (child) is not dead, but sleepeth" (Mar. 5:39); And they laughed him to scorn. These people didn't have faith in what Jesus was about to do.

Listen there will be times when you are standing on the Word of God, and people will laugh at you. But look what Jesus did—He put them all out and took the child's parents and His team members and entered where the damsel was lying. And he took the damsel by the hand and said unto her "Arise!" You must be around people that have faith and believe like you. Once Jesus put the doubters and unbelievers out, the miracle happened. Everybody couldn't go where Jesus went. He was careful about who he chooses to go into certain environments.

"Leave your father's house!" Again, for you, that could mean many things; however, whatever will hinder you from doing or receiving what God has for you, let go of it. There are those (saints) that have been around you for years, but when God starts doing a new thing in your life, jealousy, envy, and strife begins to operate in those individuals.

Peter walked with Jesus and witnessed how He handled doubters and unbelievers. So, when Dorcas had died as a result of sickness, Peter was called to come. When he arrived, he put them all forth, (he put them out) and kneeled down and prayed; and turned towards the body and said "Tabitha, arise." (Act. 9:40) Faith is not a leap in the dark; it is based on the Word of God. It is not wishful thinking, it is obedience to faith.

God wants us to stand on His promises. He said we can "...call things which be not as though they were." (Rom. 4:17) Allow the Word to work in your heart, reach out to Him. He promised He will respond to your every need. Don't be moved by what you feel, see, or hear, only by what you believe. Whose report are you going to believe, I'm going to believe the report of the Lord.

FAITH IS A SPIRITUAL FORCE!
It can push doubt and unbelief right out when we trust God.

Every accomplishment in my life came because I applied the Word of faith. I'm not moved by what I hear or see, but what I believe; I believe the Word of God. "According to your faith be it unto you." (Mat. 9:29)

The Word only works if you work it. Faith without works is dead, "What does it profit my brethren, if someone says he has faith but does not have works." (Jas. 2:14)

Let people see your faith in action.

1. Make sure you are in or connected to a Faith-Believing Church; A church that's following after Jesus Christ and equipping the people for growth and the advancement of the Kingdom.

2. Make sure you're under a Pastor who walks according to God's own heart – A spiritual father or mother that will nurture you in the things of God, who can see your potential, and who holds the keys to unleash your purpose and destiny.

"Faith is the substance of things hoped for the evidence of things not seen." (Heb. 11:1) What are you hoping for? Hope brings encouragement, expectation, and improvement. You have been waiting for a while and now it is here. God is un-leashing a force of power in you in the area of your faith.

HOPE BRINGS ENCOURAGEMENT, EXPECTATION, AND IMPROVEMENT.

We have entered a season of God's favor and greatness; His approval is upon your life and what you have been called to do. He has given you the ability to effect people and places.

"You having the same spirit of faith, according as is written, I believed, and therefore have I spoken, you also believe, and therefore speak." (2 Cor. 4:13)

You have the same spirit of who? Abraham! "And if ye be in Christ then are you Abraham's seed and heirs according to the promise." (Gal. 3:29)

You must speak the Word of God (continuously) over your situation until you see the manifestation of the thing(s) you are believing Him for. I went from receiving a welfare check of $425.00 a month to signing my own payroll checks. All things are possible if you can only believe. "Do not lean to your own understanding but acknowledge Him in all your ways and He will direct your paths." (Pro. 3:5-6)

IF FAITH IS NOT ACTIVE AND ALIVE, IT IS NOT FAITH!

When Abram was ninety-nine years old, the Lord appeared to him and said, "I am God Almighty, walk before me faithfully and be blameless." (Gen. 17:1) NIV

If you are OBEDIENT to FAITH in this season, there is a releasing of increase in your family, church, ministries, business, marriage, relationships, and friendships. The things you struggled with in the past seasons will not follow you into this new season. Speaking, Seeing and Believing releases the blessings of God.

"For all the land thou seest, to thee will I give it..." (Gen. 13:15) Take the limit off God; you are transcending beyond your own ability. "Eye have not seen, nor ear heard, neither have entered into the heart of man, the things which God hath prepared for them that love Him." (1 Cor. 2:9) "Being fully persuaded that God had power to do what He had promised." (Rom. 4:21) Whatever is in your heart to do, this is your set time (Kairos) to do it. The door of opportunity is open; walk through it! For many of you, "God has opened a door to declare His Word." (Col. 4:3)

YOU HAVE BEEN DREAMING FOR A WHILE, YOUR DREAMS ARE COMING TO PASS

"In the last days; God says, I will pour out of my spirit upon all flesh (people). Your sons and daughters will prophesy, your young men will see visions, and your old men will dream dreams." (Act. 2:17)

"The Lord shall open unto thee his good treasure, the heaven to give the rain unto thy land in his season and to bless all the work of thine hand; and thou shall lend unto many nations and thou shall not borrow." (Det. 28:12)

Prophecy: *Rise up in your strong faith and go forth to gain every victory says the Lord. Never give up.*

"Write the vision and make it plan upon the tables, that he may run that readeth it." (Hab. 2:2c) You must have a vision and believe in what you are doing even when no one else believes in you; stay away from negativity, murmuring (mutter/grumble) and complaining people. "These kinds displease the Lord." (Num. 11:1)

7

Leave people, places and things in order for you to receive! God will show you and tell you exactly what He wants you to know.

There is nothing new under the sun, God is the same yesterday, today, and forever; He revealed the new thing to Daniel, and He will reveal every detail necessary to bring the vision He has given you into fruition. "In the third year of Cyrus king of Persia a thing was revealed unto Daniel and the thing was true but the time appointed was long; and he understood the thing and had understanding of the vision." (Dan. 10:1) The Word says, "...and the thing was true..." God is not a man that he should lie, neither the son of man that he should repent, hath He said, and shall He not do it? Or has he spoken and shall he not make it good?" (Num. 23:19)

My first business started three years after I was saved. In 1983 I received my first contract with Yellow Freight Trucking Company in Newark, NJ. Everything happens in God's timing; it was three years for me, but it could be more or less than three years for you. "Wait on it, at the end it shall speak, and not lie: because it will surely come, it will not tarry." (Hab. 2:2-3)

"But the time appointed was long, and he understood the thing, and had understanding of the vision." (Dan. 10:1d) Be confident in what you know God has conceived in your spiritual womb. Don't allow doubt to enter your spirit. There may be times when it looks like nothing is happening, but you must keep moving forward, doing all that you know to do.

There are those that are with you, who will not see the vision. "And I Daniel alone saw the vision: for the men that were with me saw not the vision." (Dan. 10:7) I would speak the vision only to my family and close friends—those that were touching and agreeing with me according to the Word of God.

"I was left alone and saw the great vision." (Dan. 10:8) God is unleashing something very powerful and suddenly this season and you must be in position to receive it.

"Then he said unto me Fear not, Daniel: for from the first day that thou didst set thine heart to understand, and to chasten thyself before thy God, thy Words were heard, and I am come for thy Words." (Dan. 10:12) When the brain takes in something new, our old thought process wants to interfere. I speak over the strongholds in your thought process that is resistant to the will of God and all the new things He is birthing within your spiritual womb.

FAITH ALWAYS HAS A DESTINATION!

As you combine your faith with works, you will see every promise God has made within your heart come to pass. Faith is not a leap in the dark; it is based on the Word of God. There is no limit on what God wants to do, so you take the limit off of God. Again, God wants you to transcend beyond your ability. One can never see the thing's within them self. "Now to Him who is able to do exceeding abundantly above all that we ask or think, according to His power that work within us..." (Eph. 3:20) Incapable of being measured, indefinitely extensive. This thing is Huge; let go and let God do this. It's only through faith that you will reach the exceptional.

Faith always has a destination! A ministry that imparts the spirit of faith through preaching and teaching the Word of God, releases corporate faith.

I am releasing a fresh anointing that will activate your faith and change the way you pray and confess the Word of God. When the Word of faith is spoken, it is an opportune moment for God to move on your behalf. It is a passing instance when an opening appears, and we must drive through with force (a time to lay hold of it) if success is to be achieved—Advancing the Kingdom of God.

THEN ALL THESE BLESSINGS; ALL WHAT BLESSINGS?

"Blessed shall be the fruit of thy body, and the fruit of thy ground, and the fruit of thy cattle and the increase of thy kine and the flock of thy sheep." (Deu. 28:4)

This blessing was to the nation of Israel. But there were two covenants (contracts)—the one from Mount Sinai, which represents the bondmaid or those enslaved (represented by Hagar), and with those who are free, (represented by Sarah, the free woman). Just like Isaac, (promised and born to

Sarah) we are children of promise. Therefore, these promises are for us today. (Gal. 4:24, 26)

OCCUPATIONAL BLESSINGS

The Lord shall increase you more and more and your children. Our children and grandchildren will not have to endure the things we have gone through because of our prayers on their behalf. The Kingdom of God is going to increase more in your life. I decree and declare, you will seek the Kingdom of God and His righteousness, and all these things shall be added unto you.

- Increase In Knowledge: Revelation of things to come until the end.
- Increase In Greatness: Comfort on every side; power of wealth, and purpose. The Word of God is going to increase within you; you will have an intimate relationship with Him.
- Increase in health. All sickness and diseases have been taken away from you. "Beloved, I wish above all things that you prosper, be in health even as your soul prospereth." (3 Joh. 1:2) He wants you to be successful.

V.5 - Multiplication of Blessings: "Blessed shall be thy basket and thy store." When you are operating in faith, there is a difference between today and tomorrow. What is in your basket today will be in your store tomorrow, what's in your bank account today will be multiplied tomorrow.

V.6 - Territorial Dominion: Blessed when thou cometh in, blessed when thou goest out. God has given us supreme authority. It's like an expansion program where God puts us in charge of the production. "...Jabez prayed, Oh that you would bless me indeed and enlarge my territory..." (1 Chr. 4:10) God granted it! There is more that God has for you than what you want for yourselves. When you go into a place, you come out knowing it's yours, in Jesus name. We walk by faith, not by sight.

V. 7 - God's Protection: He secures what He gives you. Rahab took the two men and hid them. She said to the men, "I know that the Lord hath given you the land..." (Jos. 2:4, 9) You must know, that-you-know what it is that God has spoken, that He's given you.

V. 12 - Godly Favor: The time of rain is a sign of favor, activity and birthing of uncommon wealth; also, a time of promotions and open doors. Esther put on her royal apparel and found favor with the king. (Est. 5:1-2) Mary found favor with God. (Luk. 1:30) You are in a season of God's favor; the birthing time of the thing(s) which God conceived in your spiritual womb from the time you accepted Jesus Christ into your heart. "Blessed be the God and the Father of our Lord Jesus Christ who hath blessed you with all spiritual blessings in heavenly places in Christ." (Eph. 1:3)

There are five Ascension Gifts (Apostles, Prophets, Evangelists, Pastors, and Teachers) and nine Spiritual Gifts, (Wisdom, Word of Knowledge, Faith, Healings, Working of Miracles, Prophecy,

Discerning of Spirits, Divers Kinds of Tongues and Interpretation of Tongues,). Most of these gifts are lying dormant in you; they are asleep within you and need to be activated. Paul told Timothy, "…stir up the gift of God, which is in you..." (2 Tim 1:6) Which means "Activate" and as you activate the gifts within you, you will become more effective.

In verse 12, it speaks about uncommon wealth because Esther allowed God to use the gifts within her. Mordecai the Jew was next unto king Ahasuerus, and great among the Jews, and accepted by the multitude of his brethren, seeking the wealth of his people, and speaking peace to all his seed.

V. 13 - Divine Prosperity: A time when faith is demonstrated by obedience. You will prosper in every area of your life when you obey faith. Paul understood obedience to faith. (Rom. 1:5; Act. 6:7) Your confessions must be positive: "Here I am Lord! I have faith to believe. I stand on the promises of Your Word. I receive my inheritance in the name of Jesus."

- You can speak to any situation and because of the power of your tongue change occurs. Again, he said unto me, "Prophesy upon these bones, and say unto them, O ye dry bones, hear the Word of the Lord." (Ezk. 37:4)
- Speak to the dry places in your life, family, ministry, business, friendships and relationships. I decree and declare that today you will say unto these things, Hear the Word of the Lord; I am healed in my body; I am prosperous in my

finances; my home is a haven of peace; all my family shall serve the Lord.

- When you speak the Word of God, you develop your spiritual muscles to the point that there is no doubt that you won't be successful. "Build up yourselves on your most holy faith..." (Jud. 1:20) You must release your faith every day concerning those dry places; don't be moved by what you see or hear, but by what you believe.

Faith (trust in God) is the spiritual substance of the things you're hoping for and the evidence (proof) of the things you can't see. When you can't see what you want/hope to do, just ask God. (Heb. 11:1) Confessing faith (alone) is not enough; faith without works is dead. (Jas. 2:17)

Jesus asked the question: "...Nevertheless when the Son of man cometh, shall he find faith on the earth?" (Luk. 18:8b) How is faith going to be found on earth when He returns? By those who remain here on earth that are living, trusting and believing in His Word. "So, then faith cometh by hearing, and hearing by the Word of God." (Rom. 10:17)

"The Word of God shall not depart out of our mouth; but meditate day and night..." (Jos. 1:8a) You need to ponder, (consider deeply) what God is saying and doing in your life, your family, your church and business, and not take what He is saying lightly. You need to be flexible and open to change to the new ways of doing things; it is a matter of attitude and willingness to flow.

You have creative power. Use It! God created the heaven and earth, by saying, "Let there be!" All the

Words "Let there be!" in your life. "Death and Life are in the power of the tongue…" (Pro. 18:21)

Thou shall make thy way prosperous and have good success. (Jos. 1:8d-e) Some of you are waiting on God to do it for you. God's divine power has granted all things that pertain to life to you.

The key to success is Vision.

- Be clear in what you want to do.
- Research the thing.
- Ask questions.
- Team up with someone who has experience.
- Pray for and discern opportunities.
- Wait for the leading of the Lord.

Faith will bring victory. We are people on the cutting edge of God's plans and purposes; but, you must:

- "Commit thy works unto the Lord, and thy thoughts shall be established." (Pro. 16:3)
- "Demonstrate the purpose of God by being established in the faith." (Col. 1:23)
- "And the Lord shall make thee the head and not the tail, and thou shall be above only, and thou shall not be beneath." (Deu. 28:13)

Abraham transcended beyond his own ability. You must take the limits off of God and say:

- Here I am Lord;
- I have faith to believe;
- I stand on the promises of Your Word;

   In the name of Jesus, I receive my inheritance.

For He who promised, is Faithful. The Lord is not slow in keeping His promises; He said the blessings would overtake you. He has given us power to do what He promised. This is Kingdom faith. God wants the process of abundance to begin in you right now! He wants you to enjoy success now as a child of God as you move forward in faith. He wants you to "…be like the tree that is planted by the rivers of water that bringth forth his fruit in his season; his leaf also shall not wither and whatsoever he doeth shall prosper." (Psa. 1:3)

ARE YOU POTTED OR PLANTED?

"The righteous shall flourish like a palm tree; those that are planted in the house of the Lord shall flourish in the courts of our God. They can still bring forth fruit in their old age." (Psa. 92:12-14)

Are you going to grow like a cedar in Lebanon? Even when there is a drought, because you are planted, your roots are deep, and you shall not be moved. And the leaf shall not wither it will always remain green even in heated times.

Any time you trust God and are walking by faith, you are going to experience heated times. Times when you feel like giving up because of emotional, mental, or psychological pressure; times when you say, Lord where are you? And then in a still small voice He will say: "When thou passeth through the waters, I will be with you; and through the rivers, they shall not overflow thee: when thou walkest through the fire, thou shall not be burned; neither shall the flame kindle upon thee." (Isa. 43:2) "For I am the Lord thy God the Holy one of Israel, thy Savior." (Isa. 43:3a) He will never leave you or forsake you, He will be with you always, even until the end.

BEING PLANTED IN FAITH!

"But when the sun rose, because there was no deepness of earth, they were scorched, and they withered because they had no root." (Mat. 13:5-6) The health, (growth and branches) of a plant is determined by the depth and strength of its' roots. So, it is with us as Christians; we must be "...rooted and built up in Him and stablished in the faith..." (Col. 2:7a) "That Christ may dwell in your hearts by faith; that ye, being rooted and grounded in love...." (Eph. 3:17)

But you have to "leave your father's house"; that can mean people, places, and/or things. God does not bless in mess. There are those that want to live any kind of way, but the Word says, "Wherefore come out from among them, and be ye separate, saith the Lord, and touch not the unclean thing; and I will receive you." (2 Cor. 6:17) You must delight yourself in Him, and

WHATEVER IS IN YOUR HAND GOD WILL USE IT!

He will give you the desires of your heart.

How does a Christian build a root system so that the winds of change or the hurricanes of life will not uproot them? (Mat. 13:3-8) It's important that you sow your seed in good ground. Except the seed fall to the ground and die, it will never bring forth fruit. Everything starts with a seed, both naturally and spiritually.

I used my business cards as a seed; I would go from place to place and leave my card with different businesses and by faith, believed that someone would call me with a contract. And it worked.

Now faith is the substance of things hoped for, the evidence of things not seen. Whatever is in your hand, God will use it. He took the rod that was in the hand of Moses and divided the Red Sea. I don't know what it is that God has called you to do, but I do know this, He wants you to step out of your comfort zone—a place of false security.

God is calling us to transcend beyond what we could think or imagine. You must step out of the boat—you will not drown. Jesus will be with you every step of your journey. He will make the impossible possible! Oh yes, He will. He did it for me. Around 1988, I was working for a large organization. One of their programs involved housing ex-offenders who were re-entering into society. I had not earned a high school diploma or a G.E.D. but, I applied for the position to re-open this half-way house in Elizabeth, NJ. God had already granted me favor with the Executive Director of the program, so my resume was submitted to the Commissioner in Trenton, NJ. On paper, there was nothing impressive—no experience and lack of education. Somebody say, "But God!" I was in a season of God's favor. The Commissioner gave me the chance and after agreeing to several months of intensive training, by the Grace of God, I re-opened that halfway house and was able to open two more in later years.

God doesn't want you to live beneath your privileges; God is a God of increase. You are right where He wants you, seek His face. Ponder what He is doing right now. Prophesize to your tomorrow— it's going to be better than your today. I Decree and Declare the new thing that God is saying! God is releasing an Entrepreneur spirit in this season. He said, "You will be blessed, and you will be a blessing. You have the same spirit of faith as Abraham. I will direct you and provide for you."

This is a great season for the body of Christ. Revisit your vision; see what God gave you to do several years ago. For some, it wasn't built on the right foundation, so it struggled. For others, there was an interruption in what you were doing, but I hear God saying, "It is for an appointed time, rise up in your strong faith and go forth." For others, this is a time of new things springing forth; stop holding on to the old.

It's a matter of changing your attitude, dismantling the old mindset and being open to the new; understanding the times and seasons—allowing God to do this. Don't resist; don't miss God! There is a new realm of faith that we are going to walk right into. He wants to put new wine into new wine skins. Write the vision and make it plain. There will be new ministries, businesses, marriages, friendships, and relationships. You must plan ahead in all these things, in order for them to be successful.

It's simple; just believe what you hear God saying. See yourself in it; God's hand is upon it. You are going beyond the limit and rising above! You're going to surpass and achieve all that God said—**"Transcending."**

- Do not be fearful; God didn't give you a spirit of fear, but of power, love and a sound mind.
- It is a season of favor—a time when God is going to reveal everything to you.
- Don't try to figure it all out. Wait on it! The vision, it will speak.
- Combine your faith with works; you will see every promise come forth.
- Don't draw back in your faith; "Now the just shall live by faith: but if any man draw back, my soul shall have no pleasure in him." (Heb. 10:38)

These are Kingdom blessings, not the world system. Establish yourself in the faith; have confidence to trust faith. Faith sounds like a person; the scripture says we must be **"Obedient to Faith."** (Act. 6:7) Don't be like the servant that took his talent and hid it in the ground because he was afraid; his Lord called him wicked and slothful and took his talent from him and gave it to the servant who was given five talents and invested them into ten talents. His Lord gave him double. (Mat. 25:21) Whatever skills, gifts, or talent(s) God has blessed you with use them to the Glory of God.

MY DEFINITION
OF THESE PRINCIPALS OF FAITH

1. Obedience to Faith - Whatever God said or showed me I would set in my heart to do it. Not always understanding how it was going to happen, but the end results were always positive.
2. Faith is acting upon your belief in God - The more knowledgeable I am of Him, the more I trust Him. He said, "Learn of me."
3. Faith is an Action that Brings Results - If I sit back and do nothing, I will receive nothing, but when I move out in faith, I will receive what faith has for me.
4. Faith is being committed to what God called you to do - Stay focused! Distractions will throw you off course, even if what you're doing is a "good thing"; but is it what God called you to do?
5. Faith works in your heart - When we accepted Jesus in our hearts, He is Faith. The question He asks is "Will faith be found on earth when I return?"
6. You must release faith daily - Speak the Word of faith, calling things which be not, as though they are. Bringing things into their manifestation.
7. If faith is not active and alive, it is not faith - We must participate and become excited about what God is doing. Seeing things come to pass.

8. Faith is a spiritual force - All doubt and unbelief are pushed right out of your life; it cannot dwell in the same place where faith dwells.
9. Faith is in what you know - I didn't know all that I could accomplish until I heard the Word of faith. Faith cometh by hearing, hearing the Word of God.
10. We need to be faithful to all we have in Christ - No matter how small it seems to you, stay with it. If you are faithful over a little I will make you ruler over much.
11. Faith always has a destination - Faith sends you to people and places for which there is purpose; it is Apostolic in nature.
12. Faith brings victories - You never fail when you are operating in faith. You will defeat any enemy or opponent. Christ always causes you to triumph in Him.

All things are possible; you have the faith and power to move mountains, heal diseases, raise the dead, operate in the supernatural, and expel demons.

Doors of opportunity will open, walk through them. The power that energizes the Word is Faith; the power of faith is ignited by speaking boldly.

God's righteousness, His promises, and the restoration of all things will come as a result of nurturing the gifts and talents of those on your team. Your ministry/business will become stronger and greater.

Passion is more than enthusiasm or excitement; it's confidence, assurance and loving the work you are doing. It's the title deed.

When it looks as though nothing is happening, remain positive and stay focused; trust God and believe His Word. Feed your faith, starve your doubts.

Allow your imagination and your ideas to exceed to the next level. Positive words cause high vibrations; negative words cause lower frequency. This is creative power.

Set a timeframe for yourself of (approximately) six months after the start of your ministry and/or business, where you want to see spiritual, mental, emotional, physical, material, and financial growth and increase.

The substance of your ministry/business is based on faith. The Word of faith, the hearing of faith, the demonstration of faith, the life of faith, the people of faith, the power of faith, the gift of faith, and the spirit of faith. The evidence/proof that what you don't see is working for you.

There will always be delays; wait calmly on the Lord without complaining. Do not frustrate God's grace; do not seek the approval or righteousness of man, trust in Christ's finished work on the cross.

CHAPTER 2
INTENSIFYING YOUR PRAYER LIFE

Our prayers must intensify; they must become greater/stronger in order to hit the bull's-eye—this is important!

I can remember when my prayer life was weak; I just didn't think I was praying enough and now I pray three to four times a day. But it took time for me to get to this place. What helped me was getting involved on prayer lines with people who loved to pray and now I have a passion and desire to pray.

"The effectual fervent prayer of a righteous man availeth much." (Jas. 5:16b) Hear the voice of the Lord; God communicates to us through the spirit. You must pray in faith; "...faith and endurance will inherit God's promises." (Heb. 6:12b) Otherwise, when you pray, you must believe that God is going to answer your prayers and then you must wait on the answer. Don't go ahead of God by being in a hurry, thinking God didn't hear your prayer.

We must remember Daniel—a man that prayed intensely three times a day. Daniel was cast into the den of lions because he prayed; he understood that prayer changes things, people and circumstances. But Daniel's prayers were not answered for twenty-one days. However, he continued to pray and fast and make his confession known unto the Lord. And then the Lord said unto Daniel, "Fear not, Daniel, for from the first day that thou didst set thine heart to understand and to chasten thyself before thy God, thy Words were heard; and I have come for thy words." (Dan. 10:12) So, we must realize that when we pray, God hears our prayers (words) right away, but we have an enemy that tries to prevent us from receiving. The thief comes but to steal, kill and destroy—steal the words you have sent up to God. But he told Daniel I have come for your words. Hold on God hears your prayers.

Our words must line up with the will of God! "Let the words of my mouth, and the meditation of my heart, be acceptable in thy sight, Oh Lord, my strength and my redeemer." (Psa. 19:14) You must pour out your heart to God. Hannah cried out to God intensely. Here, a woman feeling less than a wife because she couldn't have children; God had shut up her womb. Many women and men today are in a state of anger, bitterness, depression and grief about different situations that they don't have answers to. But Hannah prayed unto the Lord; not only did she pray, but she made a vow (promise) to God saying, "if you give me a male child I will give him unto you all the days of his life." This is one of the reasons why we dedicate our children—we give them back to God to watch over and protect them all the days of their lives.

God began making the necessary arrangements in response to what she had asked. And before the year was out Hannah had conceived a male child. (1 Sam. 1:19-20)

I remember how angry I was at God after my daughter was killed! I felt like He didn't give me any warning. I felt so many different emotions. But it was only when I cried out intensively to the Lord that the deep anguish left. Wherever you are right now, whatever you're going through right now say, "Lord I need you to take away all my hurts, disappointments, sadness and loneliness; let thine servant fine grace and peace in thy sight."

As we live out this Christian life, we will encounter many tests and trials; but, they come to make us stronger and cause us to trust and depend on Him—not leaning to our own understanding, but acknowledging Him in all our ways, and He will direct our paths. We don't know what lies ahead of us, but God does! For you know not what you should pray for as you ought: but the Spirit itself maketh intercession for you with groanings which cannot be uttered, because He (the Spirit) makes intercession for the saints according to the will of God. (Rom. 8:26-27b)

JESUS PRAYED THEN HE WOULD ACT.

Jesus prayed, then He would act. He prayed all night before He selected the disciples. Before you make any decisions concerning anything, you need to talk to Jesus first. Most people spend less than 15 minutes a day in prayer. Our prayer life must become greater, more serious, and more extreme (Intensify). Men are to pray and not to faint; you receive victory through praying.

In Luke 18:1-8, there was a judge in a city that didn't fear God and had no regard for man. There was also a widow in that city, and she came to him asking him to avenge her adversary. He would not for a while, but she kept coming—she was persistent despite the opposition. That's what God expects from His children today, persistently praying with intense concentration on the issue(s) at hand. This is what the widow did until the unjust judge gave in to her by saying, "I will avenge her lest by her continual coming she weary me." The Lord said hear what the unjust judge said. "And shall not God avenge his own elect." We are the elect of God! "Put on therefore, as the elect of God, holy and beloved, bowels of mercies, kindness, humbleness of mind, meekness, and longsuffering." (Col. 3:12)

God chose people—calling them His children. The Lord said, "If my people, which are called by my name, shall humble themselves...; (2 Chr. 7:14) Not to be proud, thinking I don't need God, but expressing a spirit of repentance, meaning; sincere regret or remorse. For God to move on our behalf, we must "come clean", no matter what we have done or said, or thought.

If we look at the story in 2 Samuel 11-12, we see King David operating in disobedience. He was not where he was supposed to be, which as a result, caused him to fall into sin (adultery). He then tried to cover up his sin by commanding the husband (Uriah) to be placed on the front line of war, so that he would be killed because he slept with his wife who became pregnant. After Uriah's death, they were married, and she bore a son, but the Lord was displeased with the thing that David had done.

David intensively cried out unto the Lord in prayer saying, "Wash me thoroughly from my iniquity, and cleanse me from my sin; for I acknowledge my transgressions: and my sin is ever before me. Against thee, thee only, have I sinned, and done this evil in thy sight: Purge me with hyssop, and I shall be clean: wash me, and I shall be whiter than snow. Create in me a clean heart O God; and renew a right spirit within me." (Psa. 51:7) **Renew**! There was an interruption in David's spirit. I don't know what has interrupted your spirit, but things will happen in the life of a "Believer".

In 2006, I lost my daughter to an act of Domestic Violence; in 2011, I lost my son to Drugs. **Interruption**! There was a break, a pause in my life where I did sin and didn't think God was there. I couldn't pray and didn't want to read the Bible. Then one day I realized I had to let go of the anger. Be angry, but sin not. The Word also says, "And be renewed in the spirit of your mind; put on the new man, which after God is created in righteousness and true holiness. (Eph. 4:23-24) I prayed intensively. I also went to Christian counseling for eight months; it's all right to take care of your mental health as well as your physical health. Yes, as a child of God, you can battle depression. In 1 Kings 19:4-5, we find Elijah fearful, running scared, exhausted, depressed, and wanting to die. God sent an angel to touch him. The Word of God will bring you out of the worst situations, and the darkest places.

Every day submit your will and emotions to God's calling, and purpose in your life. "Let this mind be in you, which was also in Christ Jesus." (Php. 2:5) You must have a strong foundation in Christ, so when the trails and tests come, you can turn your face to the wall and pray unto the Lord saying, "Oh Lord remember me!" God remembered me at my weakest moments.

Anything you think you can't do is what God wants you to do. It's because of God's strength and your prayer. "In the name of Jesus, I decree and declare that you will love the Lord God with all your hearts, souls, strength, and minds." Jesus promised, "My grace is sufficient for thee; for my strength is made perfect in weakness." (2 Cor. 12:9) Thank you Jesus!

What the enemy tries to use against us is temptation, which will always be there in one form or another, but God will not let you be tempted more than you can bear. But when you are tempted, God will also give you a way to escape that temptation. Then you will be able to endure it. God is faithful. (1 Cor. 10:13) Paul prayed intensively; he found himself in many situations—because the spirit is willing, but the flesh is weak. He said, "For what I hate I do; for the good that I would I do not: but the evil which I would not, that I do." (Rom. 7:15, 19) It's amazing that even though you know the Word; you can become carnal-mined at some point in your Christian walk. You see, there is a war going on between the spirit man and the flesh. Paul prayed, "O wretched man that I am," (you must call it just what it is) "who shall deliver me from this body of this death," (meaning a spiritual death) sin separates you from God. "The wages of sin is death." (Rom. 6:2)

Sin is sin! There's no little sin or big sin; it's all sin. "If you say that you have no sin, you deceive yourself, and the truth is not in you." (1 Joh. 1:8) "For they that are after the flesh do mind the things of the flesh"; (**Interruption**) "but they that are after the Spirit the things of the Spirit." (Rom. 8:5) Therefore, they that are in the flesh cannot please God.

We thank God for a spirit of repentance and renewing, it keeps us from coming under condemnation. It must be true repentance— remorse/sincere regret. "There is therefore now no condemnation for them that are in Christ Jesus, who walk not after the flesh, but after the Spirit." (Rom. 8:1) "For thus saith the high and lofty one that inhabiteth eternity, whose name is Holy; I dwell in the high and holy place, with him also that is of a contrite and humble spirit, to revive the spirit of the humble, and to revive the heart of the contrite ones." (Isa. 57:15). You must cry out unto the Lord in prayer, "Create in me a clean heart O God, and renew a right spirit within me." (Psa. 51:10) "The sacrifices of God are a broken spirit: a broken and a contrite heart, O God, thou wilt not despise." (Psa. 51:17) And be renewed in the spirit of your mind. "Your body is the temple of the Holy Spirit, which is in you, which you have of God, and you are not your own." (1 Cor. 6:19)

All we must do is "Return unto the Lord: he hath torn, and he will heal us; he hath smitten, and he will bind us up. After two days will He revive us: in the third day he will raise us up, and we shall live in his sight." (Hos. 6:1-2) **GLORY!** If you believe, you will receive whatever you ask for in prayer. (Mat. 21:22)

PRAYERS YOU CAN PRAY!

1. **Supplication**: (Eph. 6:18) – Part of winning the spiritual battle is by praying at all times in the spirit with all prayer and supplication.
2. **Thanksgiving**: (Php. 4:6) – "Do not be anxious about anything, but in everything by prayer and supplication with thanksgiving let your requests be made known unto God." More examples of thanksgiving prayers are found in the book of Psalms.
3. **Faith:** (Jam. 5:15) – And the prayer of faith shall save the sick, and the Lord shall raise him up. When you pray you must believe, the conviction that life, if lived with faith in God will be our reward. Luke 18:8 asks a crucial question regarding faith, "Nevertheless when the Son of man cometh, shall he find faith on the earth?"
4. **Agreement:** (Mat. 18:19-20) – "Again I say unto you, that if two of you shall agree on earth as touching anything that they shall ask, it shall be done for them of my Father which is in heaven." For where two or three are gathered together in my name, there am I in the midst of them." Understanding the prayer of agreement: God answers united prayers—agreeing with someone of the same mindset.

5. **Worship:** The prayer of worship: (1 Chr. 16:23-24) – "Sing unto the Lord, all the earth; shew forth from day to day his salvation. Declare his glory among the heathen; his marvelous works among all nations."

6. **Warfare:** These types of prayers can be prayed in the morning:
   - (Jer. 20:13) – "Sing unto the Lord, praise ye the Lord: for he hath delivered the soul of the poor from the hand of the evildoers." (Jer. 51:20) – "I am your battle-ax and weapon of war."
   - (Psa. 16:8) – "I have set the Lord before me: because He is at my right hand, I shall not be moved." (Psa. 18:13-14) – "Lord, thunder upon the enemy; release your voice; hail stones and coals of fire. Send out your arrows and scatter them. Shoot out your light and discomfort them. (Psa. 18:40) – You have given me the necks of my enemies, and I will destroy them in the name of Jesus. (Psa. 18:50) – I am your anointed and you give me great deliverance. (Psa. 54:17) – I decree and declare that in this battle "no weapon formed against me shall prosper; and every tongue that shall rise against me in judgment I shall condemn." (Psa. 118:12) – What can man do to me. They can't over power me, they can surround me like bees. In the name of Jesus, I rebuke every demonic bee that would surround me. (Psa. 144:1) – Lord teach my hands to war and my fingers to fight.

- (Luk. 10:19) – "Behold, I give unto you power to tread on serpents and scorpions, and over all the power of the enemy: and nothing shall by any means hurt you."
- (2 Cor. 10:3-4) – "I do not war after the flesh but after the spirit. For the weapons of our warfare are not of carnal, but mighty through God to the pulling down of strongholds." This is the most powerful prayer. It brings deliverance, repentance and salvation.

7. **Intercession**: (Joh.17:6-19) - Jesus not only prayed for himself, but also for his disciples. You are to always intercede for others - family, friends, marriages, the sick, pastors, the church, co-workers (job), the lost, all those in authority, states, regions, and nations (government).

8. **Invocation:** (Psa. 25:1-5) – "Unto thee, O Lord, do I lift up my soul. Oh my God, I trust in thee....Yea, let none that wait on thee be ashamed...Shew me thy ways, O Lord....Lead me in thy truth..." You want to invoke the presence of God in everything you do.

9. **Humility:** (Luk. 18:10-14) – "Two men went up to the temple to pray, the one a Pharisee, and the other a publican. One exalted himself in prayer; the other humbled himself in prayer."
(Mat. 6:6) – "But when you pray, go into your closet, (room) close the door and pray to your Father, who is unseen." When you pray, you

are communicating with the Father; it's between you and Him. The Father knows what things you have need of before you ask Him. Jesus taught his disciples the Lord's Prayer. He said give us this day our daily bread—not just natural food, but spiritual food. Jesus knows what we need each day. If you are just coming to the Lord (newly converted/saved), you can start praying this prayer in Mat. 6:9-13.

10. **Submission:** (Mat. 26:39) – "Going a little farther, he fell with his face to the ground and prayed saying O my Father, if it be possible, let this cup pass from me; nevertheless, not as I will, but as thou will. Jesus was willing to give up his life for us. As Christian's we must understand that it isn't always about us. This walk calls for submission (willing to yield/surrender). Are you willing? "The spirit is willing, but the flesh is weak." (Mat. 26:41b) The more that you pray, you build your spiritual muscles. You may wonder, how do I do that? This is done by praying in the Holy Spirit. "But ye, beloved, building up yourselves on your most holy faith, praying in the Holy Ghost." (Jud. 1:20)

Take everything to God in prayer; prayer is the answer to all your problems and concerns. Murmuring and complaining displeases God. "And when the people complained, it displeased the Lord: and the Lord heard it; and his anger was kindled; and the fire of the Lord burnt among them and consumed them..." (Num. 11:1) You wonder why certain things are going on in your life; it is due to disobedience. Paul stated in Philippians 2:14 to do all things without murmurings and disputing— complain/grumble. Too much of this is taking place within the body of Christ today.

The results of your prayers will stop anything that is not pleasing to God. Let's not be a people with ears, but cannot hear, or eyes, and cannot see.

"I exhort therefore, that, first of all, supplications, prayers, intercessions, and giving thanks, be made for all men; For kings, and for all that are in authority; that we may lead a quiet and peaceable life in all godliness and honesty." (1 Tim. 2:1-2) We are urged to intercede intensively on behalf of our government, spiritual leaders and all those in high places. This is the Word of God; until you obey, you will never live in peace. I believe the body of Christ has dropped the ball when it comes to this prayer request from God. Why do you murmur and complain about those in office?

It's not what you or I think regarding those in authority, but God, who knows all! "And they prayed, and said, Thou, Lord, which knowest the hearts of all men, shew whether of these two thou hast chosen" (Act. 1:24). Many of you did not pray before making your decision, you acted without prayer. It is imperative that you know the power of prayer, and the effect it has in changing every situation! You can appoint or vote people into a position, but only God knows the heart of men.

"Lean not to your own understanding. In all thy ways acknowledge him and he shall direct thy paths." (Pro. 3:5-6) Remember to acknowledge God first, through prayer, before you make any decisions no matter how great or small they may be. The effectual fervent prayer of a righteous man availeth much. (Jam. 5:16) Effectual: (effective, powerful, successful in producing a desired/intended result, productive).

THE POWER OF PRAYER

Peter therefore was kept in prison: but prayer was made without ceasing of the church unto God for him. Peter was sleeping between two soldiers, bound with two chains, and guarded by four quaternions of soldiers (four squads of four soldiers each). Listen, when you have people (intercessors) praying to God on your behalf, it does not matter what the situation looks like or feels like—God is able! Peter came out of that prison successful and unharmed. (Act. 12:4-7) This is the result of people praying passionately and intensively. Many gathered together and prayed, and the Lord sent an angel to break his chains, and his chains fell off his hands.

Right now, you may feel bound by sin, or you may be in a physical prison or in an imprisoned state of mind; but we pray right now in the name of Jesus that you be set free, that every chain be broken off of you and that God will send an angel of light (a person) to minister to you. "And the prayer of faith shall save the sick, and the Lord shall raise him up;

and if he have committed sins, they shall be forgiven him" (Jas. 5:15). Some of you are sick in your bodies; the Lord said, "I am the Lord that healeth thee." (Exo. 15:26) "I will take all sickness away from you." (Exo. 23:25) "I have redeemed you from every sickness." ( ) "As your days, so shall your strength be." (Deu. 33:25) "I am the health of your countenance." (Psa. 43:5) I am Jehovah Rapha.

THE PRAYER OF SALVATION

God loves you! He loves you so much that He gave His only begotten son for you. The Bible tells us that "...whosoever believes in him shall not perish, but have eternal life." (Joh. 3:16). Acknowledge in your heart that Jesus Christ is Lord. **Repent** (be sorry, feel regret) for your sins. Make a confession with your mouth and believe in your heart that Jesus died at the cross of Calvary to take away your sins, and that on the third day He arose from the dead so that you may be forgiven of your sins and made righteous through faith in Him. Receive Him freely into your heart.

The prayer of forgiveness must be applied. There are times when someone may hurt you; and at other times, you may hurt someone. But the Bible tells us when you stand in prayer and remember that you have ought (grudge) against anyone or someone has ought against you, forgive them, so that your Father in heaven will also forgive you. (Mat. 5:23-24; Mar. 11:25-26). It's a two-way street not a one way. "Peter wanted to know how often shall my brother or sister sin against me, and I forgive him; seven times? Jesus answered seventy times seven." (Mat. 18:21-22)

"For we wrestle not against flesh and blood, but against principalities, against powers against the rulers of the darkness of this world against spiritual wickedness in high places." (Eph. 6:12) You must develop a strong prayer life. "Now I lay me down to sleep I pray the Lord my soul to keep," will not work. There are all types of spirits that come against you that you are not even aware of. A spirit of murder; this is when people are plotting and planning death, such as terrorists; you never know when or where that spirit is going to attack. Innocent men, women and children are killed because of hatred. These spirits aren't playing with you; therefore, you can't play with them. This is why the Lord gave me the Word, **Intensify**: (escalate, step up).

Praying in the name of Jesus is so powerful because when you pray in His name and with His authority, you immediately get His attention. "Elias was a man subject to like passions as we are, and he prayed earnestly that it might not rain: and it rained not on the earth by the space of three years and six months. And he prayed again, and the heaven gave rain, and the earth brought forth her fruit." (Jas. 5:17-18). When you pray intensively your prayers can change the atmosphere. This is an example of the power of prayer and your belief in what God said, "...ask anything in His name and He will do it." (Joh. 14:14). When the righteous man prays "In the name of Jesus", it can accomplish the very thing you want or need; it can stop things before they happen, and prayer lays the foundation for things to start. The more you know about who He is and who you are in Him, the more effective you are.

Jesus' teachings were "love your neighbor as yourself"—meaning all mankind, including your enemies; And having a spirit of discernment, obtaining spiritual directions.

Paul always prayed for the saints, for wisdom, revelation and knowledge. A powerful prayer he prayed was that "...the eyes of your understanding being enlightened; that you may know what is the hope of your calling, and the riches of the glory of his inheritance in the saints." (Eph.1:18) Knowing what is the hope brings expectation, excitement, and encouragement. Do you know why you were called? Christ suffered for us, leaving us an example, that we should follow His steps. That is very simple, follow the steps of Christ Jesus. Jesus did only what He saw his Father do and said only what the Father said. Jesus did nothing on his own. We need to be imitators of Christ (Joh. 5:19, 36, 14:9). Paul also prayed "...that your love may abound yet more and more in knowledge and in all judgment." (Php. 1:9) My last prayer point that Paul prayed is "...that you might walk worthy of the Lord unto all pleasing, being fruitful in every good work, and increasing in the knowledge of God;" (Col.1:1).

MY PRAYER FOR YOU:

I decree and declare multiplied blessings of increase over the lives of you and your family and all that you find your hands to do!

- The Lord shall increase you more and more and your children's children.
- I decree and declare that because of our prayers, our children won't have to go through the things we have gone through.
- The Kingdom of God is going to increase in you.
- I decree and declare that you are going to seek the Kingdom of God and His Righteousness and all these things shall be added unto you.
- You shall increase in knowledge.
- I decree and declare revelation of things to come until the end.
- You will increase in greatness and comfort on every side.
- I decree and declare power, wealth and purpose.
- The Word of God is going to increase within you.
- I decree and declare an intimate relationship with God.
- You shall increase in health.
- I decree and declare all sickness and diseases have been taken from you in the name of Jesus.

- I pray that you will be built up in your faith.
- I pray that you press through difficult situations.
- I pray for your breakthrough.
- I pray peace in every area of your life.
- I pray you walk through every open door.

WHERE DO I NEED TO BE MORE PERSISTENT?

1. Daily time with God;
2. Praying for family and marriage;
3. Sharing your faith with those that don't know Jesus;
4. Controlling your thought life;
5. Trusting Jesus with your healing and other things.

HOW DO I TRANSCEND BEYOND MY ABILITY!

Try to pray two to three times per day; set times when you will not be interrupted. Always put God first in your life; after God, it's your family. Never put your ministry and/or your business before your family; God esteems marriages highly.

"They triumphed/overcame him by the blood of the Lamb and by the word of their testimony." (Rev. 12:13). Those that are lost need to hear what Jesus has done in your life. You must cast down every vain imagination and every high thing that exalts itself against the knowledge of God and bring your thoughts into captivity. The mind is not saved.

The **Peace** that surpasses all understanding happens as a result of prayer. You will exceed in every goal that you set for yourself, your children, family, marriage ministry and/or business. Fast once or twice per week; if you can, do more; don't limit yourself.

CHAPTER 3
GRACE

Grace: The free and unmerited favor of God (dictionary of the apostolic, by John Eckhardt). Grace - Greek word Charis, meaning benefit, favor, gift. It is related to the word Charisma, meaning gratuity, endowment, miraculous faculty.

You need a wider level of acceptance and appreciation for God's grace. When I was coming up in the Lord, I heard the reason grace wasn't being taught, was that it would give people a license to sin; what foolishness! The Word states "...my people are destroyed because of lack of knowledge." (Hos. 4:6) Jesus came full of grace and truth. (Joh. 1:14c). We were saved by grace through faith; and not of yourself; it is a gift of God. This is after hearing the truth of the gospel you received salvation (Eph. 2:8).

It is crucial that we teach and preach grace. Grace causes the gifts of the spirit to operate. Also, by His grace, we can walk in unity. You are no longer a people that walk-in darkness. You are to walk worthy of the vocation where with you are called by grace.

When the people of God aren't teaching grace, they are in error; this can cause the believer to fall. Peter was reminding the believers of what they knew; "...seeing you know things before, beware lest you also, being led away with the error of the wicked, fall from your own steadfastness." He went on to say, you are sure, dependable, reliable, constant, staunch, and steady. "But grow in grace and in knowledge of our Lord and Savior Jesus Christ," (2 Pet. 3:17-18).

Grace is a gift of righteousness by Christ Jesus. Your spiritual growth is achieved by grace; it will make your life full and complete. "Being confident of this one thing, He that begun a good work in you, will carry it out to complete it." (Phi. 1:6) God resisted the proud and gives grace to the humble. Grace keeps you from being boastful; boasting is evil (Jas. 4:16). We must teach grace! The people of God are missing out on the full Word of truth. You are looking at the riches of God's grace in these teachings. Paul said to the Corinthians; "I thank my God always on your behalf, for the grace of God which was given you by Jesus Christ." (1 Cor. 1:4) "We are enriched by him in all utterance, and all knowledge; every spiritual gift was given to you by the grace of God—the word of wisdom, the word of knowledge, faith, healing, working of miracles, prophecy, discerning of spirits, divers tongues and the interpretation of tongues." (1 Cor. 12: 9) Also, there is the fruit of the spirit which is love, joy, peace, longsuffering, gentleness, goodness, faith, meekness and temperance.

The ascension gifts are Apostle, Prophet, Evangelist, Pastor, and Teacher. You possess the spirit of Wisdom, Revelation, and Knowledge; you have the keys to the Kingdom, binding and losing, and you have the anointing of God!

From the time you accepted Jesus as your Lord and Savior, these gifts were conceived in your spiritual womb. For some, they are lying dormant (asleep) within you. But I release God's grace and faith into your hearing, so that you give birth to these spiritual gifts. "Neglect not the gift that is in thee, which was given thee by prophecy, with the laying on of the hands of the presbytery." (1 Tim. 4:14) This is the impartation, a transmitted signal to wake up these gifts and to use them. "Wherefore I put thee in remembrance that thou stir up the gift of God which is in thee by the putting on of my hands." (2 Tm. 1:6) This is activation! You will become more effective when the gifts are in motion.

All these gifts are not operating in our churches. Why? It is because grace isn't being taught. You must apply grace to everything you do.

IT IS HIS GRACE THAT GIVES YOU THE ABILITY TO ACHIEVE!

Paul stated, "But by the grace of God I am what I am." Then he said, "I labored more abundantly than they all: yet not I, but the grace of God which was with me." (1 Cor. 15:10) Your degree(s), your status, who you know, and where you've been, does not matter according to the Word of God. It is His grace that gives you the ability to labor, work hard and cause you to achieve. Receive not the grace of God in vain; God has provided every tool we need to be successful. You have the grace of God in your life, so let it produce for you; don't waste His grace by doing nothing.

There are times when you may not feel adequate to fulfill the "Call". Satan will come to discourage you, interrupt you, distract you, steal from you, and destroy you. But when Paul felt weak, he cried out three times to the Lord; and the Lord responded; my grace is sufficient for you: for my strength is made perfect in weakness. DON'T GIVE UP! I hear God saying, *"I look within. As I look within, my light is going to bring forth miracles. When those that step on you, or cross you, keep moving. There is going to be full transformation in my people. When you open your mouth, I'm going to speak to the people; I AM going to release fire into them. I have called you for such a time as this. The latter rain is going to be so much greater. The people are going to know that I AM there because of the signs and wonders. I AM the Lord and I change not; fear not, I AM with thee."*

"But you have this treasure in earthen vessels, that the Excellency of the power may be of God and not of us." (2 Cor. 4:7) Excellency—a title and form of address given to a high official, such as an ambassador—one that is sent to a foreign land to represent the one that sent him.

"Now then we are ambassadors for Christ, as though God did beseech you by us: we pray you in Christ's stead, be ye reconciled to God." (2 Cor. 5:20) As an Ambassador of Christ, God's grace permits you to go boldly to the throne room, where Jesus is sitting at the right hand of the Father, where you can obtain mercy and find grace in a time of need (Heb. 4:16). You have the power, wisdom and the glory of God in you. "Behold, the kingdom of God is within you." (Luk. 17:21c). As you journey through life as an Ambassador for Christ, you are representing the Kingdom of God (His way of doing things). Therefore, it is your responsibility to mirror/reflect the sovereignty (supreme authority) of Him and take the position that you are not of this world, as He is not of the world (Joh. 17:16). This is His grace!

Jesus said, "...my Kingdom is not of this world." (Joh.18:36) The grace of God teaches you the Kingdom principles on how to operate here on earth—you are an example of Jesus. By embodying (being an expression of) the Gospel wherever you go, you live the mission of Him in the world. You are on a mission sent by Jesus Christ, the King, to advance His Kingdom. By the Grace of God, you are sent; therefore,

WE ARE WHO WE ARE BY THE GRACE OF GOD!

no weapon that is formed against you shall prosper. You are a Kingdom representative—you represent God! You are His Ambassador—His delegated authority; His voice. "Jesus is the prince of the kings of the earth. Unto him that loves us, and washed us from our sins in his blood, and hath made us kings and priests unto God and his Father." (Rev. 1:5-6) "Without the shedding of blood, there's no remission for sin..." (Heb. 9:22) Three times in these verses it refers to "us" meaning someone speaking to more than one person. Jesus is truly speaking to more than one person. This is who you are in the Kingdom of God; your identity is within Him. "And the blood of Jesus Christ his son cleanseth us from all our sin." (1 Joh. 1:7b) In whom we have redemption through his blood, the forgiveness of sins, according to the riches of his grace. Thank God for His blood. We are who we are by the grace of God. "We are a chosen generation, a royal priesthood, a holy nation, a peculiar people; that ye should shew forth the praises of Him who called you out of darkness into His marvelous light." (1 Pet. 2:9) You are no longer in the kingdom of darkness; you are in the Kingdom of light. **Know** how to operate in the Kingdom—how to look, how to talk, and how to act. **Understand** who you are in the Kingdom of God. Jesus asked Peter, "Who do men say that I am? Peter said some say you are John the Baptist, other say Elijah; and still others, Jeremiah or one of prophets? Who say you that I am? Peter answered and said Christ the son of the living God. Jesus said flesh and blood hath not revealed it to you, but my Father which is in heaven." (Mat. 16:13-17.)

It doesn't matter if people don't know who you are, or you don't belong to a large mega Church, or you're not a part of the "in crowd" as long as you are making your mark in the Kingdom of God, He knows you. Glory! To some, materialism is more important than spiritual values. Keep your perception of Christ. God is revealing to you how to advance the Kingdom of God. Make a decision to get a better understanding regarding the teachings of the Kingdom of God, which are found in the Gospels—here are a few references.

- Luk. 9:2: And He sent them to preach the Kingdom of God, and to heal the sick.

- Luk. 17:21: The Kingdom of God is within you
- Mar. 1:15: The Kingdom of God is at hand
- Mat. 6:33: But seek ye first the Kingdom of God and his righteousness; and all these things shall be added unto you.

Now let us look at what happened after the Crucifixion and Resurrection of Jesus pertaining to the Kingdom. This is crucial for you today as you move forward in the advancement of the Kingdom.

"Until the day in which he was taken up, after that he through the Holy Ghost had given commandments unto the apostles whom he had chosen: To whom also he shewed himself alive after his passion by many infallible proofs, being seen of them forty days, and speaking of the things pertaining to the Kingdom of God." (Act. 1:2-3)

The very first thing that Jesus Christ did was talk about the Kingdom of God. Why? The time and season had changed! No longer was He going to be with (among) them. However, the time had come for the apostles to prepare themselves to apply and demonstrate the things of the Kingdom which Jesus had taught them; to get ready to move progressively, and not get stuck in what they already knew.

The Second thing that Jesus Christ let the apostles know was they were going to receive Power, and then the Holy Ghost. In the Kingdom, He has given you power and you must exercise that power. "The Kingdom of God is not in word, but in power." (1 Cor. 4:20) You have the Word of God in you, and you can quote a lot of scriptures, but you must become "Kingdom-minded". This is greater than being "Church-minded". We must demonstrate the power of the Kingdom through **Miracles**—An event that appears to be contrary to the laws of nature and is regarded as an act of God, **Signs**—Something that indicates the presence of something else, and **Wonders**—Something causing amazement or awe.

After the power had been released to the apostles, Peter and John performed the first miracle when they were going into the temple to pray. A man who was lame (cripple from birth) for forty years was at the gate asking for alms. "Peter, fastening his eyes on him, along with John, said look on us. "Then Peter said Silver and gold have I none, but such as I have give I thee: in the name of Jesus Christ of Nazareth rise up and walk." (Act. 3:1-6) "Now when they saw the boldness of Peter and John and realized that they were uneducated and untrained men, they were amazed and knew that they had been with Jesus." (Act. 4:13a) These men spoke the Word of God with boldness; the power allows you to speak with boldness. As a Christian you cannot back down from teaching and preaching Jesus; you must speak the things which you know are the truth!

You must exercise your power that Jesus Christ has given you; it's not about money, cars, homes, or the size of your Church membership. It's about exercising the Dunamis (Greek Word for dynamite) power—the explosive God-given strength, ability, and power to raise the dead, such as Peter did when he was begged to come to Joppa, because Dorcas was sick and had died there. When Peter arrived, he cleared the room of those who were unbelievers; he knelt down and prayed and then told her to "Arise." She opened her eyes and saw him and sat up (Act. 9:40) You need to be in the mist of miracles, signs and wonders in your Churches today. You should be surpassing, exceeding, what your predecessors have accomplished.

As you teach the things pertaining to the Kingdom, the power of God will cause those that practice witchcraft, sorcery/divination to become a believer and follow Christ. Philip preached the things concerning the Kingdom and Simon the sorcerer believed and was baptized and continued with Philip (Act. 8) If you want to get people saved and delivered, teach the things concerning the Kingdom of God, which is the gospel (good news). The power will cause you to encounter open ways for spiritual breakthroughs. (Act. 13) When Paul and Barnabas entered the Jewish synagogue in Iconium and boldly preached the gospel, a great number of Jews and Greeks believed (Act. 14:1). The apostles demonstrated the power of the Kingdom through miracles, signs and wonders. It's simple people; but you have made this so difficult, and the unbeliever(s) aren't witnessing the power of Jesus in your life. The people of God are too caught up in materialism instead of miracles.

"Paul taught boldly in the synagogue for the space of three months, disputing and persuading the things concerning the Kingdom of God." (Act. 19:8;

26:28) And not only did God wrought miracles; but Paul almost persuaded King Agrippa, to be a Christian. Oh, such power! You have the ability to change those with other beliefs. You have the power to deliver people from the power of Satan and turn them to God. Don't under estimate who you are (your identity) in Christ. You are more than a conqueror. You must live a life full of God's power. You can't be kings and priests in the earth and not possess power.

When I was a director at a half-way house for ex-offenders, I had the power and authority to send men back to prison if they disobeyed the rules. Likewise, you must exercise your God-given power and authority in Christ as well.

We preach the rulership of God, which opens the door to all God's blessings. Whom God has called and with whom He is working His rulership through. "And hast made us unto our God kings and priests: and we shall reign on earth." (Rev. 5:10) We are called by His grace to a future of rulership, assisting Jesus Christ in His reign in the Kingdom of God; And ultimately reigning over all things (Heb. 2:6-8; Rev. 21:7).

"Then cometh the end, when he shall have delivered up the Kingdom to God, even the Father; when he shall put down all rule and all authority and power." (1 Cor. 15:24)

You are not going to have power in heaven; you need it now on earth, so use it. It's by the Word of truth, by the power of God, by the amour of righteousness on the right hand and on the left.

Jesus is seated on the right hand and the Father is seated on the left; we are sent by God's grace, so no weapon formed against us will prosper. It is a good thing that the heart be established with grace. You are to walk worthy of God, who called you unto his Kingdom and glory. (1The. 2:12; Eph.4:1)

The apostles received the things pertaining to the Kingdom of God and the power. Christ Jesus knew the challenges that the apostles would face; just like today, there's nothing new under the sun, so that's why we have the same power to deal with any situations that will arise. You see the power of preaching the Kingdom of God? It brings deliverances, healing, and salvation. It's all about the Kingdom and the grace of God.

The third thing Jesus said after his Crucifixion and Resurrection was; "…after the Holy Ghost is come upon you: ye shall be witnesses unto me both in Jerusalem, and in all Judaea, and in Samaria, and unto the uttermost part of the earth." (Act. 1:8) We are looking at the commandments given through the Holy Ghost to the apostles whom he had chosen. So, all the apostles, including women and Mary (the mother of Jesus) went up into an upper room to pray on one accord—having the same mind or purpose, in order to accomplish the will of God. This is what it will take—oneness and preaching the Kingdom, in order to advance it. "And they were all filled with the Holy Ghost, and began to speak with other tongues, as the spirit gave them utterance." (Act. 2:4) This was Jesus Christ pouring out His spirit as it was prophesied in the book of Joel.

You shall be witnesses unto me, and He names the places; this is the season of harvest. There is joy in the presence of the angels of God over one sinner that repents. Everything that we need has been provided by the grace of God to witness. "Jesus was moved with compassion on them, because they fainted, and were scattered abroad, as sheep having no shepherd." (Mat. 9:36-37) The harvest is great, but the labors are few, pray that they send labors into the field. Behold, now is the acceptable time, behold, now is the day of salvation.

There are three areas of harvest: the seed of Jesus, your seed and the seed of others (Joh. 12:23-24). First, the seed must fall to the ground; second, it must die. If Jesus of Nazareth had remained in the earth as a

THE POWER OF THE GOSPEL TRANSFORMS LIFE!

single seed, He would not have had a "body". The death and resurrection brought about viable seed. Jesus reproduces after His own kind, that's what seed does. This is why you are to be imitators of Christ.

Now he that ministered seed (your seed) to the sower, (the other person), both minister's bread for your food and multiplies your seed for sowing (2 Cor. 9:10) As you sow the Word of God, (witness to another), it just continues to reproduce, and it increases the fruit of righteousness. Before Jesus' death, He said "whoever believes in me will do the works that I do; and greater works than these will he do." (Joh. 14:12) The power of the Gospel transforms lives; it is resurrection power!

You continue to advance the Kingdom by allowing the Holy Ghost to use you just as the apostles did after they were commanded to be witnesses. In this season, you are called to Evangelize! Come out of the walls of your church; you need to be more visible. As Christians, the Lord is saying "I don't see you"; I see others knocking on doors and standing on corners with their papers; but, where are you?

You are to live the mission of Him in the world by embodying the Gospel wherever you go. You are sent by Jesus Christ and the Holy Ghost and the power of God accompanies you (Mat. 28:19-20).

Today, the Holy Ghost is your teacher here on earth to bring back to your remembrance the things that you were taught and heard. He said, "And If I be lifted up from the earth, I will draw all men unto me." You are not hearing the teachings of Jesus today; let us speak His name and get back to the Gospels. He said, "My sheep hear my voice and they follow me." People are falling away because they aren't hearing the voice of Jesus. Focus on Jesus; let Him be the center of everything you do.

We are saved to lift Him up. If you commit to teaching and preaching Jesus, you will get tangible results (Joh. 12:32; 8:28-29).

6023.That word if—in the event; on condition; there are some that will lift Him up, others will not. There is cause and effect. There is power in the name of Jesus. "And as Moses lifted up the serpent in the wilderness; even so, must the son of man be lifted up." (Joh. 3:14) We are kingdom people, so these teachings are Kingdom messages and principals which advance the Kingdom. This is about you transcending beyond your ability, taking the limits off of God and allowing him to use you in the Kingdom, not just in the Church. Being open to the "New Thing" He is showing you.

Some of our predecessors have died, in faith, not having received the promise, having seen them afar off. But God, having provided some better thing for us, that they, without us should not be made perfect (Heb. 11:39-40). Yes, everything God has promised is affirmed. Christians can rejoice in both the promises to Israel and the promises to the "grafted in" Church, which includes the death, resurrection, ascension, and return.

There are seasons of change. As 2018 was entering, the Lord spoke these three Words into my spirit: "Glory, Harvest, and Revival." I have been addressing the harvest first, because the Holy Ghost was given to witness; there are many people who are lost and waiting on you. He said go into the world and preach the gospel, pray ye therefore the Lord of the harvest, that He will send forth laborers into the harvest.

I believe that you are going to witness the manifestation of laborers; I decree and declare there will be a passion for souls like never before. I have heard thee in a time accepted, and in the day of salvation have I succored (relief from distress) you; behold, now is the day of salvation—answered prayers. You need to say **NOW** and release your faith for whomever you've been praying for to get saved and delivered. That you are not ashamed of the gospel, it is the power unto salvation. Is there salvation in any other name? Just give people Jesus, the good news that there is relief from drugs, alcohol, abuse, lust, and homosexuality just to name a few. But you can be set free in Jesus name. There are those that were brought up in the church and know the scriptures but have gone astray. All we like sheep have gone astray, went in our own way. In this season the backslider is returning back to Jesus. How shall you escape, if you neglect so great salvation; which at first began to be spoken by the Lord?

On the day of Pentecost Saul/Paul was not in the upper room. He was out causing havoc on the church, entering into every house, hauling men and women to prison and threatening slaughter against the disciples of the Lord. It doesn't matter what you have done, there is no sin whether it is past, present, nor future that Jesus can't save you from. When there is a calling on your life, Jesus will turn you around. Some of you are running right now, but in God's timing, you won't be able to escape salvation. Saul couldn't escape the voice of the Lord when he heard Him saying: "Saul, Saul why persecutest thou me"? His response was "Who art thou, Lord?" And the Lord said, "I am Jesus whom thou persecutest: it is hard for thee to kick against the prick." Once Saul's eyes became open and he received sight, he was baptized. His name was changed to Paul, and he never looked back. Paul took off the old man and put on the new. Paul understood the Old Testament teachings better than most but realized, "I am a new creature in Christ; old things have passed away, behold all things have become new." This is the attitude you must take; not looking back, but thanking Jesus for saving you, and knowing now that all the promises belong to you.

We have a new covenant with better promises; the old covenant could not save us; it could only cover our sin. The new covenant did away with our sin because of the shed blood of Jesus Christ. Receive the new wine into your new wineskins. Jesus gave a parable of trying to put on a new patch onto an old garment. The new patch will shrink/pull away the threads. The new and old cannot go together in the same way; old wineskins cannot take on new wine; it will burst. The old covenant is not compatible with the new. You are a people that are transcending beyond the old things. I will do a new thing in you, forget the former things. Paul let it be known that salvation of God was sent unto the Gentiles, for the hearts of the people is waxed gross, and their ears are dull of hearing, and their eyes have closed. Just like it is today, we must share the good news, the Gospel—preaching the Kingdom of God, and teaching those things which concern the Lord Jesus Christ with all confidence.

Sometimes you can get stuck in not knowing what you are called to do. This is the time and season for soul winning, advancing the Kingdom of God, walking in your power and authority and understanding that you are under a new covenant, with new promises.

The minds of those that believe not are blinded by the gods of this world, but the light of this glorious gospel of Christ, who is the image of God, should shine unto them. You are the image of Christ Jesus when you are sharing with them; you are giving them hope. Just think for a moment where you were when you had no hope.

God is preparing the hearts of those coming back, to receive the Word when it's spoken to them through you. "For God, who commanded the light to shine out of darkness, hath shined in our hearts, to give the light of the knowledge of the glory of God in the face of Jesus Christ." (2 Cor. 4:6) Give them the love of Jesus Christ. Love worketh no ill to his neighbor as thyself. Knowing the time, it is high time to awake out of sleep: for now, is your salvation nearer than when we believed. And to know the love of Christ, which passeth knowledge, that ye might be filled with all the fullness of God.

This is what you want for your family, friends and all those that are not saved, to be strengthened with might by the spirit in the inner man. "Let us love one another: for love is of God; and everyone that loveth is born of God, and knoweth God." (1 Joh. 4:7) There is no fear in love; perfect love casteth out fear, you are living in a time when the world is in chaos; fear is gripping the hearts of people. But you have the solution to their problem—the love of Jesus! You love Him, because He first loved you. A sinner already knows he/she is sinning; but God commanded His love toward us, in that, while we were yet sinners, Christ died for us. Amen! God so loved the world that He gave his only begotten son, that whosoever beleveth in Him should not perish but have everlasting life. Because He showed love, people from all walks of life found Him. If we teach Jesus, the love will be there. "With lovingkindness, have I drawn thee." (Jer. 31:3) God is preparing the hearts of those coming back to receive the Word when it's spoken to them. "So be ye therefore wise as serpents and harmless as doves." (Mat. 10:16) Give them the love of Jesus Christ.

Transcending Beyond Your Ability!
We are fools for Christ's sake –
But you are wise in Christ;
We are weak – But You are Strong;
We are despised – But You are Honorable!

CHAPTER 4
GOD'S GLORY IN ALL WE DO

The Greek word for Glory means doxa, "expectation" and ultimately 'glory' was used in Biblical writing to translate a Hebrew word which had a sense of brightness, splendor, magnificence, and majesty.

Glory is the brightness and splendor of God! The glory of God is like a consuming fire on the top of a mountain to the children of Israel. And the light and fire will reoccur throughout the Bible as the visible appearance of God's glory, indicating that God is both splendorous (beautiful/brilliant/exceptional) and lives in an unapproachable "light" even in this mode of self-revelation. (1 Tim. 6:16)

God's glory is His complete essence/nature—His characteristic and His mighty power being manifested through supernatural encounters. The reason we don't see more of His supernatural flow being manifested from heaven is because we are not discerning what God is releasing from the realm of glory. "The whole earth is full of his glory." (Isa. 6:3b) "God hath showed us his glory and greatness." (Deu. 5:24) "Men see not the bright light which is in the clouds." (Job 37:21)

Jesus is the only one who has seen the Father; but you will witness the glory of God in so many amazing ways as you begin to read this chapter. My prayer in writing this book is for you to see how God's Glory, Harvest, and Revival is going to usher in the greatest harvest of souls in the next few years like never before.

The voice of the Lord is powerful and is full of majesty (Psa. 29:4). He can step into our time-frame at any given time He pleases to show off His glory. The realm of the glory is timeless and holds creative power. Moses, Elijah and the Apostles subdued kingdoms, changed the weather and things pertaining to the heavens and the earth.

> ➤ "God set his bow in the cloud and it shall be for a token of a covenant between me and earth." (Gen. 9:13)
> ➤ "For I, saith the Lord, will be unto her a wall of fire around about, and will be the glory in the mist of her." (Zec. 2:5)
> ➤ "For thus saith the Lord of hosts; After the glory hath he sent me unto the nations which spoiled you: for he that toucheth you toucheth the apple of his eye." (Zec. 2:8)
> ➤ "To them (His saints) God chose to make known how great among the Gentiles are the riches of the glory of this mystery, which is Christ in you, the hope of glory." (Col.1: 26-27) ESV And when every eye sees them, they will recognize the glory of Christ in them.
> ➤ "The glory of this latter temple shall be greater than the former." (Hag 2:9)

The two ways we experience the glory of God— not in buildings, but in the hearts of spiritual Israel. The assembled body of believers also has the indwelling presence of which the Shekinah was a representation in type. This same presence is in each obedient believer, these duel aspects of the glory were seen by Zechariah who completed the Old Testament reference to these events (Zec. 8:3).

1. **Shakan**: (Lexicon Strong H7931) to protect, cover, dwell in the midst of congregation, neighborhood, or group of people in a community.
2. **Shekinah**: His Divine Presence.

These words do not appear in the Bible, but the connotation does. In the Old Testament the people were not born again; therefore, they did not have the indwelling presence of the Shekinah (Glory), so the Shakan (Glory) covered them. "And on the day that the tabernacle was reared up the cloud covered the tabernacle, and at even there was upon the tabernacle as it were the appearance of fire until morning." You are witnessing the Shakan Glory protecting the children of Israel as they journeyed. It was the appearance of a cloud pillar by day, appearance of a fire pillar by night (Num. 9:15-18). "And it came to pass, as Aaron spoke unto the whole congregation of the children of Israel, that they looked towards the wilderness and behold the glory of the lord appeared in the cloud." (Exo. 16:10)

The glory of God is like a consuming fire on the top of a mountain, to the eyes of the children of Israel. How great is God's love for his people; He said, "I will never leave you nor forsake you", but there was a time when the Shakan departed, but later returned. "And the God that hath caused his name to dwell there destroy all kings and people..." (Ezr. 6:12) The Shakan Glory had departed, and the people were not protected. There were abominations—shameful & horrible acts. "Now when these things were done, the princes came to me, saying, "The people of Israel, and the priests, and the Levites, have not separated themselves from the people of the lands, doing according to their abominations, even of the Canaanites, the Hittites, the Perizzites, the Jebusites, the Ammonites, the Moabites, the Egyptians, and the Amorites. For they have taken of their daughters for themselves, and for their sons; so that the holy seed have mingled themselves with the people of those lands..." (Ezr. 9:1-2)

God is always there to protect you if you obey Him. You see what happens when His covering is lifted. "Our iniquities are increased over our heads, and our trespass is grown up unto the heavens." (Ezr. 9:6)

"Thus saith the Lord of hosts; I was jealous for Zion with great jealousy, and I was jealous for her with great fury. Thus saith the Lord; I am returned unto Zion, and will dwell in the midst of Jerusalem..." (Zec. 8:2-3) The key Word is dwell. You are looking at the Shakan Glory it covers and protects groups of people. "...There shall yet old men and old women dwell in the streets... And the streets of the city shall be full of boys and girls playing in the streets thereof." (Zec. 8:4-5) Our streets will be safe again from the drugs, gang violence, etc. Shakan Glory is watching over them.

"Speak ye comfortably to Jerusalem, and cry unto her, that her warfare is accomplished, that her iniquity is pardoned, for she hath received of the Lord's hand double for her sins. And the glory of the Lord shall be revealed, and all flesh shall see it together." (Isa. 40:2;5).

Don't fall into the hands of an angry God, even though you are under the dispensation of Grace. He's the same yesterday, today and forever, just waiting on you to show up in the streets—in your troubled communities; the Shakan Glory will usher the loss right into the house of safety. The Shakan shows up in dark places and brings light. There was always a leader, a spokesperson. You need to show up, so God can show out.

In the Old Testaments times the people would be covered by the glory or anointed/gifted for a specific service or task. "The spirit of the Lord God is upon me" (Shakan Glory) "because the Lord hath anointed me to preach good tidings unto the meek; he hath sent me to bind up the broken hearted, to proclaim liberty to the captives, and the opening of the prison to them that are bound." (Isa. 61:1) God is always concerned, always there to supply whatever you need. "Then a cloud covered the tabernacle—the tent of testimony, and the glory of the Lord filled the tabernacle. When the cloud was taken up, the children of Israel could continue on their journey, but if the cloud wasn't taken up, they journey not; they rested." (Num. 9:15-18) Your foot steps should always be ordered by the Lord; if He says go, then go; if He says stay, than stay. You get into trouble when you don't follow the leading of the Spirit of God.

The Shakan also was present and at work in the New Testament. "Peter, James and John were taken up into a high mountain with Jesus, and behold a bright cloud overshadowed them: and behold a voice out of the cloud which said, this is my beloved Son, in whom I am well pleased; hear ye him." (Mat. 17: 5) They witnessed what you and I can experience here on earth according to His Word.

"The glory of the Lord has risen upon you", (Shakan) "The earth shall be filled with the knowledge of God's glory." When you come to understand that you operate from a supernatural realm, you will witness the manifestation of God's presence.

"Who shall ascend into the hill of the Lord? Or who shall stand in his holy place?" (Psa. 24:3) It's an environment that Jesus was careful about whom he took with him. Everyone is not going to the hill; everyone is not going to see what God shows you.

"Lift up your heads, O ye gates;" you are the portal/gate entrance-way for God's glory to come into the earth and then to witness to the loss; "ye everlasting doors; and the King of glory shall come in." Jesus Christ is the door into the gospel. "He that entereth not by the door into the sheepfold, but climbeth up some other way, the same is a thief and robber. But he that entereth in by the door is the shepherd of the sheep." (Joh 10:9)

"I will fill this house with glory; the glory of this latter house shall be greater than of the former", there's was a transition from one to the other. From the Shakan Glory covering you, to the Shekinah glory that dwells within you. "And the latter house is greater. "Greater is He that is in you, than he that is in the world." This transition took place when you were translated from darkness (came from the world) into His marvelous light (came to Christ—born again). Everything in the latter house is greater—it surpasses the former. You have a better covenant, better promises; this is how I interpret it. "He has made us ministers of a new covenant, not of the letter but of the spirit; for the letter kills, but the spirit gives life."

New wine in new wine skins, yes, we are under the influence of the Holy Spirit, which is the new wine that Jesus paid for with his blood (Act. 2:13). If you try to put a new patch onto an old garment, the new patch will shrink and pull away the threads. The new and the old cannot go together. The old covenant is not compatible with the new covenant. You cannot be saved by the old wine/old covenant; the only way a person can be saved is by Jesus Christ (Act 4:12). The old covenant only covered sin; the new convent takes away sin. This cup is the new covenant in my blood which is poured out for you.

The apostles witnessed the latter house glory and Peter recorded it. "For we have not followed cunningly devised fables, when we made known unto you the power and coming of our Lord Jesus Christ but were eyewitnesses of his majesty. For he received from God the Father honour and glory, when there came such a voice to him from the excellent glory, This is my beloved Son, in whom I am well pleased." (This omniscient eternal presence of the Almighty is the heavenly, not the earthly). "And this voice which came from heaven we heard, when we were with him in the holy mount." (2 Pet. 1:16-18)

Another example of the Shakan Glory, in the New Testament; the hour had come where Jesus predicted his crucifixion to the people. "Father glorify thy name. Then came a voice from heaven saying, I have both glorified it, and will glorify it again. The people therefore, that stood by heard it, said that it thundered: others said, an angel spake to him. Jesus answered and said, this voice came not because of me, but for your sakes." (Joh. 12:29-30) People, communities, and congregations, the Shakan Glory, will show up on their behalf, it will cover, it will speak; it will demonstrate the power of God. This is how the unbeliever knows that there is something different about you; it's by the life you live before them, not just on Sundays, but also by the works you do and the light of God's glory that shines brightly through you. "For God who commanded the light to shine out of darkness hath shined in our hearts, to give the light of the knowledge of the glory of God in the face of Jesus Christ." (2 Cor. 4:6) When God spoke and said, "let there be light" and it was so, he gave you the supernatural and creative power to speak to every person that's in darkness and give them the knowledge that they can be transformed into his marvelous light. Glory!

The fruit of the earth is going to be reconciled back to God. During the years of 1948-1952, there was a revival called the Latter Rain. During that time its' emphasis was relational networking; however, it died down after a few years. The emphases regarding these two Words Glory and Harvest is going to usher in a great revival. This revival will bring about repentance, reconciliation, and restoration. The outcome is defeating the powers of darkness and advancing the Kingdom of God. In order to be prepared for this revival, we must hear the voice of God and follow His directions. "Today, if you hear his voice, harden not your hearts." (Heb. 3:7-8) You are in a time of preparation. God is getting his church/Ecclesia ready. He's restoring your passion for souls, and your love for the things of Christ—the drive you once had.

Prophecy: And the Lord said; you were heading in a specific direction but got off course and became distracted and because of this, your mind and emotions were agitated but, healing, and deliverance are yours. Be renewed in the spirit of your mind in Jesus name. You must be healed to bring wholeness to others.

God wants to dwell with his people, his glory will be so strong that all they will have to do is walk in the midst and every need will be met, by the spirit of God. When the Apostle Peter passed by, his very shadow would fall on the people and they were healed. So the people would bring the sick out into the streets to be healed.

You are in a season of healing, miracles, and faith. These three are the spiritual power gifts of God. These are important, because "the Kingdom of God is not in Word only, but in demonstration of the spirit and of power." (1 Cor. 2:4) "God wrought special miracles by the hands of Paul." (Act. 19:11) When you go forth and preach the gospel to every creature, the Lord will work with you confirming the Word with signs following. Jesus demonstrates his glory through these spiritual power gifts here on earth in you. This is your season, your time of purpose to be fulfilled.

Revelation	Power Gifts	Speaking Gifts
Word of Wisdom	Faith	Speaking in Tongues
Word of Knowledge	Gifts of Healings	Interpretation
Discerning of Spirits	Working of Miracles	Prophecy

In the natural there are four seasons—Winter, Spring, Summer, and Fall. They all are different in their representation. Some of you look forward to some of them, others you can't wait until some of them are over.

In the supernatural you have seasons, and times for every purpose under heaven. Understanding the times and seasons allows you to move strategically. The purpose of God's glory (presence) is for the light to shine on the harvest of souls that they may be saved. He is positioning his people that have been called for this very purpose. Your call comes from His purpose. "Who hath saved us, and called us with a holy calling, not according to our works, but according to his purpose and grace." (2 Tim.1:9a) When you hear the voice of God speaking to you to do certain things, know that it's already in you. It originates from Him.

"Before I formed you in the womb I knew you." (Jer. 1:5) Each season frames your purpose. I am in the season and time of God's purpose for my life. How do you know your season?

Well I can only tell you what I heard Him say to me when I asked the same question— you understand and know what His calling for you is through prayer, fasting and seeking His face.

> "Then shall you call upon me, and you shall go and pray unto me, and I will hearken unto you." (Jer. 29:12)
> "The steps of a good man are ordered by the Lord." (Psa. 37:23)
> "And we know that all things work together for the good, to them that love God, to them who are the called according to his purpose." (Rom. 8:28)
> "The plans and thoughts God has for you are thoughts of peace, and not of evil, to give you an expected end." (Jer. 29:11)

Get in position and agreement with his purpose. You can't live your call unless you know your purpose, it requires time with God. Only

YOUR PURPOSE IS TO CARRY THE GLORY OF GOD!

the pure in heart shall see God! The purer you are, the more vision you receive. Your purpose is locked up within your heart. "Where your treasure is, **there** your heart will be also." (Mat. 6:21) Purpose is the reason for existence; it is the outcome of a thing. Your purpose is to carry the glory of God; it is the self-expression of the Kingdom of God in you. Don't let frustrations and discontentment set in. Find that one thing that makes you feel alive, and you will know that's your "**there**."

Purpose means pleasure of God in you; a valuable thing; desire; a delight; the Shekinah glory; his divine presence; A divine call to serve, and to walk worthy of it. "You are workmanship created in Christ Jesus unto a good work which God hath before ordained, that you walk in them." (Eph. 2:10)

So, no matter what people said about you, you didn't understand why you had to go through, but His grace and mercy leads you to your purpose. You were designed on purpose for His purpose we are to fulfill His purpose in the earth. Every day you need to realign your mind, will, and your emotions to the purpose of God.

Again, this is the season for God's Glory, Harvest and Revival to manifest. So, everything that I do, I concentrate on the purpose and plan of God concerning the revival. The more I share with men and women of God what He is saying to me, I get more and more confirmation that He is speaking the same thing to them—this is a season for revival!

God wants His glory to be manifested through you in the same way; you are His workmanship, created in Christ Jesus unto a good work even greater works God will perform through you, but you must trust Him, have faith to believe in what He's called you to do, and move in it. Your faith should not stand in the wisdom of man, but in the power of God.

> ➤ "You are to walk worthy of the vocation wherein you are called. That you would walk worthy of God who called you unto his Kingdom and glory." (Eph. 4:1; 1 The. 2:12)
> ➤ "But we have this treasure in earthen vessels, that the Excellency of the power may be of God and not of us." (2 Cor. 4:7) The Shekinah glory is manifested directly through us, rather than externally, through the cloud or fire.

Infinite—endless/limitless it's only in these that the Shekinah glory is now manifested. "For you are the temple of the living God, I will dwell in them, and walk in them, and I will be their God and they shall be my people." (2 Cor. 6:16b) God's spiritual presence is dwelling in you. We need a sovereign move of God's divine presence.

Every time Moses came out of the presence of God, he had to put a veil over his face because of the brightness. The veil is abolished; it was done away with in Christ. "Much more doth the ministration of righteousness exceed in glory." (2 Cor. 3:7-9) Oh how much more will the ministry of the spirit, be not more glorious in you. This is what transcending beyond your ability is about—exceeding and surpassing what our predecessors had.

> ➤ "But if our gospel be hid, it is hid to them that are lost: In whom the god of this world hath

blinded the minds of them which believe not, lest the light of the glorious gospel of Christ, who is the image of God should shine unto them that are in darkness. The Divine presence of God and the glory of God in you are going to usher in the harvest of souls." (2 Cor. 4:3-4)

➢ "But we all, with open face beholding as in a glass the glory of the Lord, are changed into the same image from glory to glory even as by the spirit of the Lord." (2 Cor. 3:18)

What do you see when you look into a glass or mirror? God's glory cannot be hidden! When every eye sees you, they will recognize the glory of Christ in you. "To whom God would make known what is the riches of the glory of His mystery among the Gentiles, which is Christ in you, the hope of glory." (Col. 1:27) There are no more mysteries to them that are filled with the spirit of God—you are the hope to a dying world! "For God, who commanded the light to shine out of darkness, has shined in our hearts, to give the light of the knowledge of the glory of God in the face of Jesus Christ." (2 Cor. 4:6) This is God's purpose!

God's purpose for your life is that you prosper—be successful, flourish, especially financially. It's amazing how when you live in alignment with purpose, God blesses every area of your life. He spoke to my spirit the latter part of last year about teaching on Facebook Live; I never thought about it before, but it turned out to be my **there**, along with writing this book. Purpose is about the nature of which you are, it's about being who God called you to be—your characteristics and temperament. In order to fulfill your purpose, you must become a new creature in Christ, old things have passed away and all things have become new. Purpose is not in doing but being.

"Martha, Martha, thou art careful and troubled about many things"; (worried) Martha was busy doing, doing, doing, she was cumbered about much serving, meaning she was over occupied with the care of business which distracted her. Martha asked Jesus to "bid Marry to help her." (Luk. 10:40-41) Let no one pull you out of your purpose. When you are doing, doing, and doing and not being who God called you to be, it causes frustration, and discontentment in you. Your hopes and desires aren't being fulfilled, you have become restless almost to the point that you feel God as forsaken you. But He hasn't; He said, "I will never leave you nor forsake you." You are just doing things that are not giving God the glory. You need to return to your first love, He will heal you; He will revive you, and on the third day He will raise you up and you shall live your spiritual life again—your devotional time, quiet time, a special retreat, a place where your soul can catch up with your body.

Mary sat at the feet of Jesus and heard the Word; she understood where she needed to be. Being where you are supposed to be, keeps your focus on your purpose. "Jesus said one thing is needful; and Mary hath chosen the good part which shall not be taken away from her." (Luk. 10:38-42) Mary was in fellowship with Jesus, she listened to what He was saying, she understood what was important in life— the things that matters the most. This was the same Mary that took her expensive perfume and she poured it on Jesus' feet, and wiped His feet with her hair.

Knowing your purpose gives you confidence to move in the supernatural and no matter how foolish it may seem, God takes that to confound the wise; and God has chosen the weak things of the world to confound the things that are mighty.

I was working on a job where I was spending more time there, then with Him. God allowed that job to close down to get my attention. God is a jealous God; sometimes you put other things before Him as I did. Your purpose is not a job (it is bigger than these things): career, vocation, degree, etc. it is independent of all those things. This is why you give God all the glory; "It's not by might, nor by power, but by His spirit that dwells in you"—His very presence (Eph. 3:16) that He would grant to you, according to the riches of His glory, to be strengthened with might by His spirit in the inner man.

Understanding your purpose puts you back on track. David got way off track by committing sin; but God knew from his mother's womb that he would become a man after God's own heart. Once he repented, God forgave him. David wrote, "One thing have I desired of the Lord, that will I seek after; that I may dwell in the house of the Lord all the days of my life, to behold the beauty of the Lord, and to inquire in his temple." (Psa. 27:4) Purpose brings you into the presence of God. What are you doing? A lot of you are busy for the Lord, but are you being who He created you to be?

The fruit of your labor is being who God purposed you to be when He called you. If you are just doing and there's nothing to show for it, you are out of your season.

To everything there is a season; naturally and spiritually. Each natural season has its own representation, winter does what it does, and summer, spring, and fall do the same. Spiritually, God can speak to you and give you a directive, instruction or impregnate you. And he will let you know when your season is to come forth or give birth.

2018 is a great year for the saints of God. It's a season and time to move out in the things of God. It's a season and time of grace and favor; it's a time when God spoke to my spirit about these three Words Glory, Harvest, and Revival. God's purpose for your life—it's not about doing, but about being. I began writing this book in January 2018 and it will be published before December 31, 2018.

Obedience to the voice of God and the move of God is imperative. It's the season and time of opportunity; it's your Kairos time; meaning propitious/favorable, a moment for a decision or action to take place; the opportune or appointed time that God has set for a thing to occur. On March 12, 2018 I did a teaching on God's timing; I said you will never walk into your purpose if you don't understand the timing of God. A few hours later, I released the first announcement on social media that Glory, Harvest, and Revival are coming in 2018 to the East Coast—Get ready! I have no idea what God is about to do, all I know I was born for His purpose. It's all about souls! The harvest is great, and the laborers are few. Dominion—meaning "supreme authority" is what I heard in my spirit some time ago in 2007 concerning the East Coast Revival. This revival was pertaining to the governors and their states and the emphasis were on Salvation, Deliverance and Restoration. Now, eleven years later it's coming to pass. God is still dealing with me about revivals the "Glory, the Harvest and Revival. ***Prophecy:*** *Over the next three years we are going to witness some of the greatest revivals and they are all going to concentrate on souls.* Recently, In August 2018 I watched the Revival Harvest America in Olean, New York on television where attendees witnessed God's miracles as 15 people who were blind received their site and many souls received salvation and deliverance. Also, in that same month in the city of Newark, New Jersey the Festival Of Life Revival touched the hearts of thousands and over 3000 souls were Saved. God's grace and favor is now upon the things that seemed to be difficult or impossible in the past. **Never give up on what you know you heard God say to you**. Your favor is in the sphere of your purpose. Who are you influencing?

Esther walked in her purpose; when she entered the king's chambers, she obtained favor. "And the king loved Esther above all the women, and she obtained grace and favor." Why? Because the window of opportunity was open for her to save her people. It was Esther's Kairos moment for decision and action. Esther moved in the time zone of God. When you do, it's a good and favorable chance of success. We see this throughout the book of Esther.

Timing is every bit as important as the cause; it is when time and purpose comes together. That's how you achieve your goals.

> ➢ Times—signifies, points out and expresses
> ➢ Seasons—signifies the characteristics of the duration of time. The quality of the person, place and thing.

Jesus was born in the fullness of time—the perfect time for Christ birth, at the decisive moment. The God-ordained census required Mary and Joseph to leave Nazareth and to go to Bethlehem at the exact time Jesus was to be born. Why? So that he would be born in the city that was prophesied in scripture. (Gal. 4:4)

In releasing the presence of God, you are now giving unto the Lord the glory due his name. We just entered a new time zone; everybody **THERE IS FAILURE IN UNDERSTANDING THE FLOW OF GOD!** may not understand why, but we must accept it because we cannot change it. It is the same with the Word of God. "A wise heart discerneth both times and judgment." (Ecc. 8:5b) There is failure in understanding the flow of God; it is time we tune our frequency to the time zone of God.

"Come and let us return unto the Lord: for he hath torn, and will heal us; he hath smitten, and he will bind us up. After two days will he revive us; on the third day he will raise us up, and we shall live in his sight." (Hos. 6:1-2)

This is a season of God's favor; we are not talking about a few acts. There is much in scripture regarding the "third day" let us explore a few. As we press deeper into the third day and read these verses, let us personalize them. Are you experiencing, or have you experienced a third day in the Lord? Significant things will happen in your life as you step into your third day in the Lord.

> Luke 13:32 (NIV): And he said unto them, Go ye, and tell that fox, behold, I cast out devils and I do cures today and tomorrow, and the third day I will reach my goal. **The Word of God states that in the third day <u>He</u> will raise you up. Not your husband/wife, your children, your family/friends nor your leader. But <u>He</u> will!**

> Genesis 1:9-13: The earth was created—**we have power.**

> Genesis 22:1-5: Abraham's ultimate test. **Where is your there?**

> Exodus 19:9-11: God's major appearing to all of Israel. **Don't miss the move of God in your life.**

- ➤ Luke 9:22: "Saying, The Son of man must suffer many things, and be rejected of the elders and chief priests and scribes, and be slain, and be raised the third day." **God wants to restore and replenish some things in your life.**
- ➤ Esther 5:1-2: Esther put on her royal apparel and found favor with the King. **Are you presenting your body as a living sacrifice holy and pleasing to God?**
- ➤ John 2:1-11: Jesus launched into his ministry of miracles; water was turned into wine. **Allow the Lord to use you—it is a time for miracles, signs, and wonders.**
- ➤ Matthew 16:21: "From that time forth began Jesus to shew unto his disciples, how that he must go unto Jerusalem, and suffer many things of the elders and chief priests and scribes, and be killed, and be raised again the third day." **Keep your mind on the things of the Lord and not of men.**
- ➤ Isaiah 60:1: Arise, shine; for the light is come and the glory of the Lord is raised upon thee. **The Glory, Harvest, & Revival are apostolic Words in nature; they will affect change across geographic lines because they have a specific mission. He said keep teaching on my glory, the labors will come as a result.**

This is a season that God is revealing and exposing those things that are operating in darkness.

The spirit of the Lord is upon us, to preach, teach, pray, heal, deliver and set at liberty those that are brokenhearted, captive, blind and bruised. This is the acceptable year of the Lord. There are souls waiting to be snatched out of sin; there is no more hiding from the things God has called you to. Walk in your purpose and "give unto the Lord the glory due unto his name; worship the Lord in the beauty of holiness." (Psa. 29:2) It's all about His Kingdom; His Power; His Glory; Forever!

CHAPTER 5
THE POWER WITHIN YOU!

The meaning of transcending is: to go beyond the range or limit of a thing that has been followed or replaced by another current person; to surpass; exceed; excel; climb or overshadow.

In this last chapter you will be exploring all of these meanings of this Word and discover where you are today in the process. Transcending Beyond Your Ability is based upon Ephesians 3:20: "Now unto him that is able to do exceeding abundantly above all that we ask or think, according to the power that worketh in us."

There is failure in understanding the flow of God; you must flow in the right spirit, you must flow with a new perspective, and you must look at things differently. It is time you tune your frequency to God's time zone.

Thank God for the new covenant. "You are a chosen generation, a royal priesthood and a holy nation, a peculiar people; that you should shew forth the praise of him who hath called you out of darkness into his marvelous light." (1 Pet. 2:9) Your position is that you are to surpass your predecessors, or forerunners, and exceed what they did. Jesus said, "...greater works than these shall he do; because I go to the Father." (Joh. 14:12c) You must believe that greater things are still to come; the great commission – "Go you therefore and teach, all nations, baptizing...I have commanded you; I am with you always even until the end of the earth." (Mar. 16:14-

85

18) This is yet to be accomplished, and Jesus will not return until everyone knows of Him. "Give ear, O ye heavens, and I will speak; hear O earth, the Words of my mouth." (Deu. 32:1) You are to proclaim the doctrine upon the earth, it shall fall like rain.

Heaven will supply your needs to sow seeds into the hearts of those that don't know Him. Rain is not from man, and the soil is ready for a miracle. He is the Rock, His work is perfect. You are to teach God's Word like never before, He's going to show Himself strong on behalf of those whose hearts are perfect towards Him. What do you value more, earthly things or heavenly things? Your attention will be wherever your treasure is. "Sanctify the Lord God in your hearts" and be ready always to give an answer to every man who asks you a reason for the hope that's in you..." (1Pet. 3:15) Keep your heart pure from rituals. People are looking for something that they feel works. As I stated previously, you are transcending, not going back into bondage; the finished work of Jesus Christ is perfect.

"Now faith is the substance of things hoped for, the evidence of things not seen." (Heb. 11:1) People are living without hope today, and God wants to use you to bring hope to a dying world. The feelings and expectations should be that something is going to happen because God said so. You must not use trickery—witchcraft. Yes, unfortunately, these things are prevalent in our churches today. People are prostituting their gifts by charging money for a prophetic Word, and other ungodly things are taking place "In the name of the Lord." God has supernaturally anointed you to teach and preach the unadulterated Word of God. His anointing causes you to destroy yokes, preach deliverance and set the captives free, opens prison doors, preach the gospel to the poor, heal the brokenhearted, recovering of sight to the blind, and to set at liberty to them that are bruised (Luk. 4:18).

I saw a wave in the spirit; in that wave were people, and they were getting healed and delivered. God was breathing upon the people, and the glory (Shakan) was hovering over them. The glory was so heavy that the people could barely stand. All they could do was weep and lay out before Him until it lifted. His voice said, "I have come to revive my people." "In these lay a great multitude of impotent folk, of blind, halt, withered, waiting for the moving of the water", these were sick, lame people. "For an angel went down at a certain season into the pool and troubled the water: whosoever then first after the troubling of the water stepped in was made whole of whatsoever disease he had." (Joh. 5:3-4) It was their time.

Confirmation: *A testimony was shared with me about a phenomenon which had occurred on March 18, 2018 at a women's conference, where after the Woman of God had finished preaching and left the room, God moved so mightily that nobody was left standing."*

In this season and time, God is sending a wave of water which represents His spirit to heal, deliver and revive; and on the third day, He will raise them up and they shall live and not die. Saints you are right there! You are witnessing the very breath of God in the earth, giving mouth to mouth resuscitation; when you speak, touch or just pass by, your presence will cause miracles. Many of you are hearing the voice of the Lord saying, "Whom shall I send? And who will go for us?" (Isa. 6:8b) and many of you are thinking, what should I say or do? He commanded Ezekiel to prophesy to the dry bones, to live. He's commanding you to prophesy to the lost souls, that Jesus died that you may live. It's not by might, or by power, but by the spirit of God that is in you.

GOD IS RAISING UP NEW PROPHETIC VOICES IN THE EARTH TODAY!

God is raising up new prophetic voices in the earth today. People who never prophesied before are going to hear the voice of God speaking to them, and they are going to speak prophetically what He's saying and showing them. Say with me, "Here I am Lord, send me!" It's crucial that you know where you are and where God is taking you. Commit your works unto the Lord, and thy thoughts shall be established. In all your ways acknowledge Him, and He shall direct your path.

Jesus gave His apostles priesthood authority while he was with them on earth that would enable them to do the same works they had seen Him do. The disciples/apostles didn't have the Holy Spirit in them as you and I today. "These things have I spoken unto you, being yet present with you. But the comforter, which is the Holy Spirit, whom the Father will send in my name, he shall teach you all things..." (Joh. 14:26) I am speaking about transcending—overshadowing and outdoing.

Stop limiting yourselves; God is revealing strategies on how to defeat the powers of darkness and you are a part of this great time. You are the light of the world. "And all things are of God, who hath reconciled you to himself by Jesus Christ, and hath given to you the ministry of reconciliation." (1 Cor. 5:18) What I am saying is you have a great testimony! Your testimony is your ministry! Ministry does not only take place in the pulpit. Your mindset must change, and you must expect greatness; therefore, walk in His authority with no intimidation. "And they overcame him by the blood of the Lamb, and by the Word of their testimony." (Rev. 12:11)

> **YOUR MINDSET MUST CHANGE, AND YOU MUST EXPECT GREATNESS!**

"Now has come salvation, and strength, and the Kingdom of our God, and the power of his Christ..." (Rev. 12:10) But the greater works that you and I can do is result of his death, burial, resurrection, and ascension—they brought about viable seeds to reproduce and transform lives; the Lord of the harvest is doing this. Now the hour has come that you are witnessing people getting healed and Saved in the hospitals and other places where it's unexpected. Millions of people have accepted Jesus Christ! When Jesus walked on earth as a man, He was only able to be at one place at a time. However, you have the ability to reach people around the world through social media/social networking, television, radio, telephone, Skype and you're your mode of transportation. Social networking was not available during His time here on earth as it is for you today. This is how we have exceeded our predecessors. If Jesus had remained in the earth as a single seed as Jesus of Nazareth, He would have remained as the only spirit-filled person in the earth—a Head without a body; "Now you are the body of Christ, and each one of you is a part of it." (1 Cor. 12:27 NIV)

God's ordained census required Mary and Joseph to leave Nazareth and go to Bethlehem at just the time when Jesus was to be born. Why? So that he would be born in the city that was prophesied in scripture. In the fullness of time God sent forth His son; a perfect time for Christ's birth, at the decisive moment. Everything is in God's timing. "Transcending Beyond" is understanding progression as you study the Bible.

- ➢ The story in John 5:5: A man who had an infirmity for thirty-eight years, was there at the pool waiting for someone to put him into the pool after the healing waters had been troubled.
- ➢ Moving forward in our study of the Bible in James 5:15: "And the prayer of faith shall save the sick and the Lord shall raise him up."

Can you see the progression? You don't have to wait; all you need is to have faith when you pray. Utilize every available tool that God has placed in your hands. Your personal inadequacies don't matter. If you want to be used by God, seize the moment; no looking back, no procrastination.

Today, there is no excuse for not reaching the lost. God wants you to be visible; He wants to see you out in the fields. "Lift up your eyes, and look on the fields; for they are white already to harvest." (Joh. 4:35b) Souls are so ripe to the point of readiness for harvesting. Seeds have already been planted and watered. It's God that gives the increase. "Now he that Planteth and he that watereth are one: and every man shall receive his own reward according to his own labor." (1 Cor. 3:5-9). What will your reward be according to your labor? "For you are co-workers in God's service; you are God's field, God's building." (1 Cor. 3:9).

The fire shall try every man's work of what sort it is. The requisition is soul winning. I tell you, "There is joy in heaven over one sinner who repents, more than over ninety and nine just persons, which need no repentance." (Luk. 15:7) "And my soul shall rejoice in the Lord, it shall exult in his salvation." (Psa. 35:9) There is a call to Repentance; I believe the key to advancing the Kingdom of God is repentance! The more you witness and share the love of Jesus, the more the atmosphere will be filled with the spirit of Repentance. Those who are thinking wrong thoughts will be convicted.

THESE ARE THE ENEMIES OF TRANSCENDING!

1) **Fear**: Repent from fear - Confess all of your fear before the Lord and ask Him to forgive you for entertaining this demon; then, get a hold of it and cast it out. Make it go by the strength of your will.

2) **Rebellion**: Repent for rebellion - Confess it and ask God to forgive you; then, cast out a deaf and dumb spirit, you can identify it by the confusion it brings to your mind.

3) **Rejection**: Repent for rejection (receiving rejection and for rejecting others). Confess it and ask for forgiveness; then, cast out the spirit of the antichrist—this spirit is against everything that is pure and holy.

4) **Unforgiveness**: Repent for unforgiveness – confess all unforgiveness and ask God to forgive you; then release and forgive everyone who has hurt you or came against you in any way. Then, cast out the spirit of infirmity which keeps you hopeless, disabled, unable, and sick.

5) **Resentment**: Repent for resentment - Confess all areas of resentment and ask the Lord to forgive you and release you; then, cast out a spirit of jealousy.

6) **Witchcraft**: Repent for witchcraft - Confess your desires and efforts to control others through your attitudes and behavior. If you have ever been involved in the occult, reading horoscopes, playing with Ouija boards, or

anything else, repent and ask the Lord to forgive you; then, cast out a spirit of divination.

7) **Pride**: Repent for pride. Cast out a haughty spirit.

8) **Hypocrisy & Deception**: Repent for hypocrisy and deception - Cast out a lying spirit that has caused you to live in fantasy.

9) **Idolatry**: Repent for idolatry - Confess all areas where you have put people or things ahead of God; then, cast out a spirit of whoredoms.

10) **Lust**: Repent for lust - Whether it be sexual, or greed and/or a desire for approval and attention; then, cast out unclean spirits. These usually come in groups, so make them all go.

11) **Defilement**: Repent for defilement for the ungodly places you've been, and for the things you've seen, heard or read; Repent for entertaining pornography and all that goes with it; then, cast out a perverse spirit.

12) **Bitterness**: Repent for bitterness - Release all hurt and injury from the past. Ask God to forgive you for being a victim of life's circumstances, instead of taking your proper position of being victorious in Christ; then, cast out a spirit of bondage.

13) **Discontentment**: Repent for discontentment - Cast out a seducing spirit that has seduced you into wrong attitudes and behavior.

14) **Heaviness**: Repent for depression, discouragement, disappointment – then, cast out a spirit of heaviness.

15) **Death**: Repent for laziness, procrastination, a desire to die, for wanting to give up, etc. Then, cast out a spirit of death.

Now, ask the Lord to fill all empty places with His precious Holy Spirit and forbid those demon spirits to come back. Do not entertain the things that you have repented of again. Feed yourself on the Word of God daily and stay in prayer.

People that are not Saved are worthy of our prayers. Prayer will give birth to revival, revival will give birth to repentance, repentance will give birth to reconciliation, and reconciliation will give birth to restoration.

Reconciliation: An end to a conflict or separation.

How do you move from repentance/forgiveness to being reconciled? Forgiveness is always required by God, but it does not always lead to reconciliation. Reconciliation is a process. Why? Say you have a son or daughter who is on drugs, and they keep stealing from you to support their habit. They keep asking for forgiveness saying, "I'm sorry, I won't do it again", but they continue to do it repeatedly. Hurt and damage are building up inside of you. Even when that time comes when they genuinely repent and are remorseful, it's hard for you to trust them again. It is a process. At the same time, they must accept the fact that their actions have caused you hurt, harm and pain, and that it will take time for you to be healed. Thank God, Jesus Christ is not like you or me. I forgave the man who killed my daughter; although he is no longer alive, I don't think I would have reconciled with him. "And you, that were sometime alienated and enemies in your mind by wicked works, yet now hath he reconciled and given the ministry of reconciliation." (Col. 1:21; 2 Cor. 5:18)

The fruit of the earth is going to be reconciled to God. "The earth is the Lords and the fullness there of and all that dwell within." (Psa. 24:1) What we are about to witness is not a onetime event, but a movement that God has placed in my heart to see souls come to Christ.

Restoration: Rebuild, rise up, repair and restore. The Lord promised to restore to you everything the enemy has stolen from you.

Your walk with the Lord will be better; some of you have gotten hurt in the service of the Lord. For your shame, you shall have double. "I will restore to you the years that the locust hath eaten, the canker-worm, and the caterpillar and the palmer-worm, my great army which I sent among you." (Joel 2:25) He wants you to have joy, and health in your body; He will return you back to your former owner. "You were bought with a price: (by the Blood of Jesus) therefore, glorify God in your body, and in your spirit, which are God's." (1 Cor. 6:20)

I AM calling you out! I called Adam out after he fell into temptation, "And the Lord God called unto Adam, and said unto him, Where art thou"? (Gen.3:9) There are souls waiting to be called out of their sins; they are tired of their lifestyle. There is no more hiding from the things I have called you to. Walk in your calling. You will witness people from all walks of life, returning unto God. "He leadeth you beside the still waters." (Psa. 23:2b) Still waters are the new place(s)—the new thing that God is leading you to. As you flow in the "still waters", you will receive spiritual growth, peace, purpose, and motivation.

Prophecy: *The glory of God is being called forth, it has been held captive, the glory will break off the chasing of darkness and the light and the glory are now coming forth. Chuck Pierce - October 2, 2009*

Prophecy *"Keep teaching on my glory; the laborers will come as a result." For I will pour water upon him that is thirsty, and floods upon the dry ground; I will pour my spirit upon thy seed, and my blessings upon thine offspring. The glory will usher in a new move; a visitation, and then the harvest. It is for such a time as this, a right-now time when God is breathing His breath upon the face of the earth.*

> ➤ "So shall my word be that goeth forth out of my mouth; it shall not return unto me void, but it shall accomplish that which I please, and it shall prosper in the thing whereto I send it." (Isa. 55:11) You are transcending; this is the time of God's favor; Rise up and Rebuild!
> ➤ "And you shall be called the repairer of the breach; The restorer of paths to dwell in." (Isa. 58:12)

➤ "…'In the time of my favor I heard you, and in the day of salvation I helped you.' Now is the time of God's favor, now is the day of salvation." (2 Cor. 6:2)

➤ "Say to the prisoners, Go forth; and to those that are in darkness; Show yourselves." (Isa. 49:9)

➤ "Where sin abounded, grace did much more abound." (Rom. 5:20b)

➤ "Your lips have been anointed with grace" (Psa. 45:1) to speak over sin.

➤ "Your tongue is the pen of a skillful writer." (Psa. 45:1g)

Prophecy: *I AM opening great doors in every area of your life and you cannot be ignorant or allow Satan to take advantage of these opportunities. For you are not ignorant of his devices. A great door and effectual one is open.*

Because of the shed blood of Jesus Christ, you have won the victory over Satan and his kingdom and every demonic force; however, war is still waging for souls! God has given you authority and power to expose Satan's tactics and to overcome his attacks. You have dominion over the earth realm. Satan has set himself up to be god in the earth, which makes him an Imposter! He is seeking who he can steal, kill and destroy in any kind of way. But the God of peace shall bruise Satan under your feet shortly.

SPIRITUAL PRINCIPLES FOR TRANSCENDING

> **Recognize**: The starting point is really recognizing that God is sovereign. He is, was, and will always be in control. (1 Pet. 4:11-12)
> **Remember**: Bring to mind the truth of what God has said, but also what God has done. His love, faithfulness and even his discipline. (Heb. 10:23)
> **Faith**: Is our response to what God directs. It is founded on our relationship to God's authority and our position in the Kingdom of God. (Rom. 10:17)
> **Focus**: Is where your attention is centered; an essential spiritual principal. The Bible directs you to maintain your focus on Jesus Christ and eternity. (Isa. 26:3; Heb. 12:2)
> **Love**: When you engage in loving others we engage in actions that build them up. Demonstrations of love outweigh the actions of harm. The Bible encourages us to love others, especially those that are poor or in unfortunate circumstances. (1 Joh 4:18)
> **Uplifted**: You must choose to uplift Him; it's a hard thing to do in difficult times. It involves surrendering yourself. You are to stand firm for a reason. Uplifting God with praise and worship is an ongoing, continual process, setting aside you, and giving Honor where it is due. (Heb. 13:15)

- **Rest**: This principle is powerful; however, you often fail to recognize the importance of rest. Transcending only occurs when you are able to be at a place of rest. People really have a hard time entering rest or even understanding it. Resting is all about coming to a settled state, where there is no striving to obtain. (Heb. 4:9)
- **Stability**: Being still before God and waiting patiently on Him. A spiritually stable person is a person who is firm in godly character; they are fixed or steadfast in godliness. (Php. 4:1)
- **Integrity**: Comes from within the heart. Moral principles. And herein do I exercise myself, to have always a conscience void of offence toward God, and toward men. (Act. 23:1; 24:16)
- **Trust**: Everyone who has been given much, much will be required. And from the one who has been entrusted with much, much more will be asked. (Luk. 12:48)
- **Humility**: Is about serving; It's not about being above. Instead whoever wants to become great among you must be your servant. (Mat. 20:27)
- **Unity**: Let nothing be done through selfish ambition or conceit, but lowliness of mind let each esteem others better than himself. (Php. 2:3-4)
- **Joy**: Now the God of hope fill you with all joy and peace in believing, that ye may abound in

hope through the power of the Holy Ghost. (Act. 15:13)

> **Patience**: But let patience have her perfect work, that ye may be perfect and entire, wanting nothing. (Jam. 1:4)

> **Wisdom**: If any of you lack wisdom, let him ask of God, that giveth to all men liberally, and upbraideth not; and it shall be given him. (Jam. 1:5)

"He (Christ) ascended up far above all heavens, that he might fill all things." (Eph. 4:9-10. Because of Christ's ascension, you are able to transcend (to raise yourself beyond, to climb) being filled with all the fullness of God. "Now unto him that is able to do exceeding abundantly above all that ye ask or think, according to the power that worketh in you…" (Eph. 3:20) Going beyond measure, the height and dimension is hard for some to comprehend. Therefore, you limit God; but God lives in a dimension outside of limits or time. Paul refers to four different dimensions—what is the breadth, and length, depth, and height. When you talk about the spiritual realm there are multiple dimensions (Eph. 3:18).

Abraham was given dimension, which a measurement of size of something in one or more directions, i.e. breadth, length, depth, or, height. This word dimension used in the plural denotes the whole space occupied by a body. Gen. 12:1-5 (the call); 14:19 (possessor); 15:5 (vision); 17:1-9 (promise).

- ➢ **Breadth** – The measurement from one side to the other;
- ➢ **Length** - The distance from end to end;
- ➢ **Depth** – The measurement from the top of something to its bottom;
- ➢ **Height** – The distance between the lowest and highest point of something.

God appeared to Abram at ninety-nine and began to teach him the Kingdom long before Jesus came and started teaching the Kingdom. "I will make my covenant between me and thee; and will multiply thee exceedingly; you will be a father of many nations; And I will make thee exceedingly fruitful; you will be established, and I will give unto you the land wherein that art a stranger... for an everlasting possession." (Gen. 17:2-9) Dimension is the ability to do and to have in the earth that which is in heaven; from the deepest point in the earth, to the highest point in heaven. You must be spiritually minded; you cannot receive this in the flesh.

"According as he hath chosen you in him before the foundation of the world, that you shall be holy and without blame before him in love." (Eph. 1:4) God, who manifested himself in the flesh as Jesus, came and gave you the same opportunity to have Kingdom dimension. What you must understand is that you are already blessed with all spiritual blessings in heavenly places in Christ and have obtained an inheritance. Christ ascended above all heavens that He might fill all things; He has given to the church, which is His body, the fullness of Him that filleth all in all.

Your prayer is that "The eyes of your understanding being enlightened; that you may know what is the hope of His calling, and what are the riches of the glory of his inheritance in the saints." (Eph. 1:18) and that you will move and become possessors of Kingdom dimension. This is the glorious church. You must know how to surpass normal, physical, and human experiences. By praying this prayer, you need to receive a transcendental (a spiritual/non-physical) level of knowledge, so that you can enter into heavenly realms and receive the blessings that God has for you that are not subject to limitations. "God raised Christ from the dead and

BEING SEATED WITH CHRIST IS HIGHER THAN STANDING!

seated Him at the right hand in the heavenly places. He put all things under his feet and gave Him as head over all things to the church, which is his body, the fullness of him who fills all things." (Eph. 1:20-23) "And hath raise us up, (you and I) together, and made you sit together in heavenly places in Christ Jesus; that in the ages to come He might shew the exceeding riches of His grace in his kindness toward you through Christ Jesus." (Eph. 2:6-7) God raised us up with Christ and seated us with Him in heavenly realms in Christ Jesus. Being seated with Christ is higher than standing; the believer has been elevated to a position that is far superior to the angels. "But to which of the angels did God say at any time, sit at my right hand (together with me in royal dignity)?" (Heb. 1:13-14) AMP. When a person of high rank and authority puts someone at their right hand, that person is given equal honor with him and is recognized as a possessor of equal dignity and authority. The right hand symbolizes Jesus, the Messiah possessing the power and authority to subdue His enemies. (Psa.18:16; 110:1; Mat. 22:44)

Our citizenship is in heaven, this is where you are and where you belong. You don't have wait for your physical body to be reunited; the reality is that your spirit is already united. That's why you must set your minds on things above, not on earthly things; build your hopes on things eternal. What belongs to Christ also belongs to you. You are united; it's like a marriage. What you obtain in the marriage belongs to you and your spouse – it becomes community property. So, you are joint heirs with Jesus Christ.

When the Holy Spirit spoke to me saying, "2018 was the year for the body of Christ," I began to speak what I heard the voice of the Lord saying, and many took heed. I am witnessing the prophecy manifesting itself through Ministries, businesses, marriages, Healing Revivals, books, etc. It's about delighting yourself in the Lord and He's giving you the desire(s) of your heart. The keys are being obedient and acting in faith. He said, "Don't worry about money or anything pertaining to what I called you to do this year; you are the bride of Christ!"

Unfortunately, there are those who don't have ears to hear, and eyes to see what God is saying or doing. These are the doubters, procrastinators and unbelievers. I'm referring to operating in the supernatural realm, and therefore, the doubters, unbelievers, the procrastinators, etc. are not going to receive the keys to the kingdom.

We're talking about the third dimension, the realm where God resides. This is the spiritual world that I've been talking about. You are already blessed with all spiritual blessings in Heavenly places in Christ Jesus. All you have to do is turn, speak and believe that anything you ask in his name shall be given to you. Turn spiritually, not naturally.

The prayer of binding and loosing is so important because it says, "Whatsoever you bind on earth shall be bound in heaven, and whatsoever you loose on earth shall be loosed in heaven." (Mat. 18:18) If you are seated in the third dimension in the heavens where God is, and you need something down here on earth, you must learn how to use the prayer of binding and loosing. For instance, if I need finances to support the Ministry, I will pray, "Father I bind here on earth anything that will hinder the finances that I need for the Ministry and thank You that it is bound in heaven, and I loose the finances needed for the Ministry on earth, that You shall loose them from heaven in Jesus' name. Amen!" That is how you release through the prayer of binding and loosing, and you receive it that way. When I started praying this way, God revealed to me that I was not to worry about anything that I need, just do what He asks of me to do. Prior to that, I had a tendency of trying to figure out how am I going to do this or that?

Matthews 16:19 says, "And I will give unto you the Keys of the Kingdom of Heaven: and whatsoever thou shall bind on earth shall be bound in heaven; and whatsoever you loose on earth shall be loosed in heaven." You have the keys to go in and out; you have access. It's just like in your home where you live, you have keys. Everybody does not have a key to the door of your home, but Jesus has given you the keys to heaven and you can go in and out through binding and loosing.

In Matthew 20:23 Jesus said, "Ye shall drink indeed of my cup, and be baptized with the baptism that I am baptized with: but to sit on my right hand, and on my left, is not mine to give, but it shall be given to them for who it is prepared of my Father." Again, we're looking at being seated on the right hand, and here also on the left; you are again, in that third dimension where God is, and you will be seated with Him right there; He has given you access to the throne room. Glory to God!

I believe that I am right where God wants me to be in this season. I didn't understand at first, how we would transfer from the third dimension to the other dimension. The more I studied the Word of God, the more the Lord revealed His will to me, and that is when I realized that all the blessings are right where you and I are seated, in that third dimension with Him. For years I wondered about the scripture: "A good man leaveth an inheritance to his children's children: and the wealth of the sinner is laid up for the just." (Pro. 13:22)

It's not about trying to transfer to the other dimension, we already have it. You just have to believe by faith and move out when the Lord speaks. He told me this year was a year for the body of Christ, anything you need is available to you. When I said I believe that I'm right where God wants' me, I am experiencing and witnessing that as soon as I spend money pertaining to the Ministry or writing this book, immediately, God touches the heart of someone to replace the money I've spent. It's according to his riches in Christ Jesus! This is not complicated at all, it's just about getting into the Word, allowing the Spirit of God to open up (to reveal) to you exactly what He is saying and what He is showing you, and then moving without hesitation.

I believe that's where you make a mistake because you try to figure this thing out and you end up making it too complicated, instead of it being easy as 1, 2, 3.

Our predecessors didn't have the rhema (written) Word before them as you have it today, therefore, you must transcend – overshadow and exceed what they did. Since you have access to the written Word, you have the ability to actually sit with the Word of God and allow the Holy Spirit to bring the Word to Life (logos). As we get an understanding, it makes it much easier for us to surpass the things that our predecessors did.

I pray that clarity is coming to you as you're reading and getting an understanding of how transcending works. It's all about praying the prayer of binding and loosing; it's about being obedient to faith and realizing that you can accomplish so much more because of who you are in Christ Jesus. Once you get a hold of something and you know it's good, it's just like tasting something that's good. David said, "Oh taste and see that the Lord is good..." (Psa. 34:8) Well, we are tasting the goodness of Jesus Christ; We are capable of doing and receiving these things only because of Him; He causes us to transcend beyond our ability. "Behold I will do a new thing: now it shall spring forth; shall you not know it?" I will even make a way in the wilderness and rivers in the desert." (Isa. 43:19)

This all started for me last year when God gave me the scripture Isaiah 42:9: "Behold, the former things are come to pass, and new things do I declare: before they spring forth I will tell you of them." The Lord not only tells me about the new things, but also shows me the new things. God is so faithful, and I just want to encourage you that He is no respecter of persons; the same things that He has done for me, He wants to do for you. "For it is God which worketh in you both to will and to do his good pleasure." (Php. 21:13)

God is producing in you both the desire and the ability to do the things that pleases him. He said to us, "Fear not little flock, for it is your Father's good pleasure to give you the kingdom." My Brothers and Sisters in Christ, **Transcending Beyond Your Ability** is God's good Pleasure!

Transcending occurs only when you are able to be in a place of "**Rest**." This principle is powerful, but you often fail to recognize the importance of rest. People really do have a hard time entering rest or even understanding it. Resting is all about coming into a settled state where there is no striving to obtain. "There remaineth therefore a rest to the people of God. For he that is entered into his rest, he also has ceased from his own works, as God did from his." (Heb. 4:9-10)

God created the Heaven and the Earth in six days, and on the seventh day he rested from his labor. The problem with the body of Christ today is we don't know how to stop, be still, and hear from God. I remember when I did not know how to rest; I thought it was all about being busy, busy, busy, but once I understood it, I came to a place where I could hear God and was able to move forward. "Let us labor therefore to enter into that rest, lest any man fall after the same example of unbelief." (Heb. 4:11) Wow! If you don't come to a place of rest, you are laboring in vain and you could fall just as if you were an unbeliever. As Believers, we must enter into God's rest! "For we which have believed do enter into rest, as he said, As I have sworn in my wrath, if they should enter into my rest: although the works were finished from the foundation of the world. For He spake in a certain place of the seventh day on this wise. And God did rest on the seventh day from all His works. And in this place again, if they shall enter into my rest. Seeing therefore it remaineth that some must enter therein, and they to whom it was first preached entered not in because of unbelief." (Heb. 4:3-6)

Unbelief and disobedience hinders you from transcending! "According as his divine power hath given unto us all things that pertain unto life and godliness, through the knowledge of him that hath called us to glory and virtue: Whereby are given unto us exceeding great and precious promises: that by these ye might be partakers of the divine nature, having escaped the corruption that is in the world through lust. And beside this, giving all diligence, add to your faith virtue; and to virtue knowledge; And to knowledge temperance; and to temperance godliness; And to godliness brotherly kindness; and to brotherly kindness charity. For if these things be in you, and abound, they make you that ye shall neither be barren nor unfruitful in the knowledge of our Lord Jesus Christ. But he that lacketh these things is blind, and cannot see afar off, and hath forgotten that he was purged from his old sins. Wherefore the brethren, give diligence to make your calling and election sure: for if you do these things, ye shall never fall: For so an entrance shall be ministered unto you abundantly into the everlasting kingdom of our Lord and Savior Jesus Christ." (2 Pet. 3:11)

ENDORSEMENTS

Apostle Ruth Parker is an outstanding communicator, with an effortless style; unveiling truth in such a way, as to draw the reader on a journey of Discovery and encounters of the ability of our God. I love the title of this book – Transcending Beyond Your Ability! When the believer knows who he is in Christ, he will know what he has and what he can do through Christ. Col. 2:9-10, "For in him dwelleth all the fullness of the Godhead bodily. And yes, are complete in him, which is the head of all principality and power." Everything in HIM is good. Active recognition of this truth must dominate your thinking, because that is truly who you are in Christ. The challengers around the believer do not define him; he is defined by his position in Christ.

Apostle Benjamin Arazu
River of Life Church
Rome, NY

Apostle Parker informed me that she had been led by the Spirit to write a book; when she told me the title "Transcending Beyond Your Ability", I was fascinated. I knew that it was definitely given by the Holy Spirit, because this is not her natural vocabulary. She has faced many emotional and spiritual challenges which, as I know today, were a springboard to upward mobility in Christ. Using the metaphor of the eagles, from time to time they go through a process called molting. This is a time of weakness and vulnerability; but when they come through, they are renewed like a young bird again. Having the age and experience, they are better.

When we go through our struggles, (molting) and wait upon the Lord, we will come forth with renewed strength. (Isa. 40:31)

Rev. Dorothy Smith
At The Crossroads of Life Ministry
Union, NJ

"Transcending Beyond Your Ability" is a book that is a "must read" and "best seller." Apostle Parker is my Pastor, Mentor, Spiritual Confidant and friend. I've been working closely with her as her assistant for many years and have witnessed her to transcend beyond her abilities. She is a true woman of God, a woman of faith and a mother in Zion who hears from God. She has the God-given ability to see your God-given gifts and talents that are lying dormant and cause them to awake and arise. As you read this book, you will be challenged and encouraged to soar.

Pastor Renee' Cummings
Have God-Will Travel Ministries
Linden, NJ

BIOGRAPHY

How It All Began

In April of 1980, an eighty-two-year-old Mother explained to me that Jesus had snatched me right out of sin. The things that I was engaged in a few days before (the drugs, alcohol, cigarettes, and lust), I was unable to continue doing. He had supernaturally cleansed me. I wasn't attending any church at this time; Mother gave me a Bible and said to me, "wait on the Lord, He will direct you."

At this point, if you haven't made the Lord your Savior, you might want to stop right now ask the Lord into your heart, just say, "Jesus please forgive me of my sins, cleanse me from all righteousness, come into my heart and live in me from this day forward, in Jesus' name. Amen! (Rom. 10:9)

While reading the Bible, I allowed the Holy Spirit to teach me; there were Word meanings and pronunciations that I didn't understand. After six months, He directed me to attend a Church called Victory Temple, which later became the Christian Bible Institute, under the direction of the late Dr. Donald Womack, located on Springfield Avenue in Newark, New Jersey, where I served as a lay member for seven years.

After the first two years of listening and absorbing the Word-of-Faith teaching and learning how to trust God, I began to operate in faith. (Rom.

10:17) "Faith cometh by hearing, hearing the Word of God"!

In 1982, I established my first business – E.C. Janitorial Service. From 1992 until 2013, I was the Pastor of Jesus Cares Ministry; and I also owned and operated Link-2-Link Business Network, and Just Care for Children. In 2013, Apostolic Builders Ministries International was birthed. (Jam. 2:14-17) "Faith without works is dead."

www.ingramcontent.com/pod-product-compliance
Lightning Source LLC
Chambersburg PA
CBHW071131090426
42736CB00012B/2089